How To Construct
Achievement Tests

How To Construct Achievement Tests

Fourth Edition

Norman E. Gronlund hp: (619) 451-0315
University of Illinois

ALLYN AND BACON
Boston London Toronto Sydney Tokyo Singapore

Library of Congress Cataloging-in Publication Data

Gronlund, Norman Edward, (date)
    How to construct achievement tests.

    Rev. ed. of: Constructing achievement tests.
3rd ed. cl982.
    Includes bibliographies and index.
    1. Achievement tests—Design and construction.
2. Examinations—Design and construction. I. Gronlund,
Norman Edward, (date)   Constructing achievement
tests. II. Title.
LB3060.65.G76 1988   371.2'61   87-1280
ISBN 0-13-402181-9

To
Marie Ann Gronlund
and
David, Derek, and Erik

Contents

Preface

How to Construct Achievement Tests is a practical guide for constructing informal achievement tests. Like earlier editions, this fourth edition is intended for teachers, prospective teachers, and others engaged in test construction. It takes the test constructor through the various stages of test planning, item writing, test assembly, test administration, and the interpretation of test results. A chapter on validity and reliability is added at the end of the book, for those who want to examine the technical bases for effective test construction and use.

This edition differs from the first three editions in a number of ways. (1) The four chapters on constructing test items (Chapters 3–5) have been reorganized to put greater emphasis on how to construct each item type. (2) Sample test items have been added to the rules for writing true-false and short answer items to illustrate application of the rules. (3) New sections on ''Computer Use in Testing'' and ''Using a Test Item File'' have been added to Chapter 7. (4) A new section on standard scores has been added to Chapter 8. (5) The section on validity in Chapter 9 has been rewritten to fit the latest APA *Standards* which view validity as a *unitary* concept. In addition, a ''Summary of Points'' and new references have been added to each chapter.

Because of its practical orientation, special efforts were made to keep the writing simple, direct, and understandable to persons without prior knowledge of measurement or statistics. The numerous sample test items used to illustrate effective item writing are based on the content of the book to show how specific content can be fashioned into test items. Sample test items in other subject areas can be obtained from the references listed at the end of each chapter.

My appreciation is expressed to the authors and publishers referred to in the text, to Irene Palmer for her excellent typing, to the Prentice-Hall editorial staff, and to my wife, Marie, for her patience and assistance.

Norman E. Gronlund

How To Construct
Achievement Tests

1

Achievement Testing and Instruction

Well-designed achievement tests support and reinforce other aspects of the instructional process. They aid both the teacher and the student in assessing learning readiness . . . monitoring learning progress . . . diagnosing learning difficulties . . . and evaluating learning outcomes. . . . The effectiveness of testing is enhanced by careful attention to the principles of test construction and to the use to be made of the results.

All types of instructional programs can benefit from the effective uses of achievement tests. In regular classroom instruction, achievement testing can serve a variety of useful functions. In individualized instruction, mastery learning programs, and the use of computer-assisted instruction, achievement testing is an indispensable procedure for monitoring and directing learning. Despite the widespread use of achievement testing and the important role it plays in instructional programs, however, many teachers receive little or no instruction in how to construct good achievement tests. This book is an attempt to correct that deficiency. It places major emphasis on those principles and procedures of test construction that are useful to classroom teachers. A guiding theme throughout the book is that achievement testing should be an integral part of the teaching-learning process.

An achievement test is *a systematic procedure for measuring a representative sample of learning tasks*. Although the emphasis is usually on measuring a set of *intended* learning outcomes, as defined by the instructional objectives, it should not be implied that testing be limited to the end of instruction. All too frequently, teachers view achievement testing as an end-of-unit or end-of-course activity that is done primarily for the purpose of assigning grades. Although this is one useful function of testing, it is just one of many. As with all teaching activities, the main purpose of testing is to improve learning and it can contribute to this end in a number of ways.

TESTING IN THE INSTRUCTIONAL PROCESS

In order to realize the full potential of achievement tests as learning aids, it is necessary to make testing an integral part of the instructional process. Testing should be considered during the planning for instruction, and it should play a significant role in the various stages of instruction. From the beginning of instruction to the end there are numerous decisions that teachers must make. Testing can improve the effectiveness of many of these decisions by providing more objective information on which to base judgments.

Let us consider three types of decisions teachers need to make that can be aided by testing: (1) decisions at the beginning of instruction, (2) decisions during instruction, and (3) decisions at the end of instruction. Doing so will also help acquaint us with the names of the test types that are typically associated with each stage of instruction.

Beginning of Instruction (Placement Testing)

There are two major questions that teachers need to answer before proceeding with the instruction:

1. To what extent do the students possess the skills and abilities that are needed to begin instruction?
2. To what extent have the students already achieved the intended learning outcomes of the planned instruction?

Information concerning the first question can be obtained from *readiness* pretests. These are tests given at the beginning of a course or unit of instruction that cover those prerequisite skills necessary for success in the planned instruction. For example, a test of computational skill might be given at the beginning of an algebra course, or a test of English grammar might be given at the beginning of a German course. Students lacking in prerequisite skills could be given remedial work, or they could be placed in a special section that had lower prerequisites.

The second question can be answered by a *placement* pretest covering the intended learning outcomes of the planned instruction. This might very well be the same test that is given at the end of the instruction; preferably it should be another form of it. Here we are interested in determining whether students have already mastered some of the material we plan to include in our instruction. If they have, we might need to modify our teaching plans, encourage some students to skip particular units, and place other students at a more advanced level of instruction. The function of placement testing is summarized in Figure 1.1.

Placement testing is, of course, not always necessary. Teachers who have worked with students for some time may know their past achievements well enough

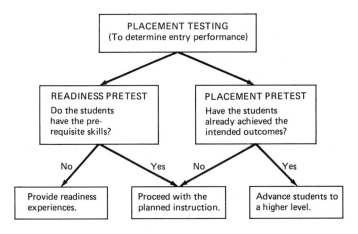

FIGURE 1.1. Simplified Model for the Instructional Role of Placement Testing.

that a pretest at the beginning of an instructional unit is not needed. In other cases a course or unit of instruction may not have a clearly defined set of prerequisite skills. Similarly, some areas of instruction may be so new to the students that it can be assumed that none of the students have achieved the intended outcomes of the planned instruction. Placement testing is probably most useful when the teacher is unfamiliar with the students' skills and abilities and when the intended outcomes of instruction can be clearly specified and organized in meaningful sequences. Under these conditions the placement test provides an invaluable aid for placing each student at the most beneficial position in the instructional sequence.

During Instruction (Formative and Diagnostic Testing)

During the instructional program our main concern is with the learning progress being made by students. Questions such as the following must be answered:

1. On which learning tasks are the students progressing satisfactorily? On which ones do they need help?
2. Which students are having such severe learning problems that they need remedial work?

Tests used to monitor student progress during instruction are called *formative* tests. Formative tests are typically designed to measure the extent to which students have mastered the learning outcomes of a rather limited segment of instruction, such as a unit or a textbook chapter. These tests are similar to the quizzes and unit tests that teachers have traditionally used, but they place greater emphasis on (1) measuring all of the intended outcomes of the unit of instruction, and (2) using the results to improve learning (rather than to assign grades). The purpose is to identify the students' learning successes and failures so that adjustments in instruction and learning can be made. When the majority of students fail a test item, or set of items, the material is typically retaught in a group setting. When a minority of students experience learning failures, alternate methods of study are usually prescribed for each student (for example, reading assignments in a second book, programmed instruction, and visual aids). These corrective prescriptions are frequently keyed to each item, or to each set of items designed to measure a separate learning task, so that students can begin immediately after testing to correct their individual learning errors.

When a student's learning problems are so persistent that they cannot be resolved by the corrective prescriptions of formative testing, a more intensive study of the student's learning difficulties is called for. It is here that the *diagnostic* test is useful. This type of test typically includes a relatively large number of test items in each specific area with slight variations from one item to the next so that the cause of specific learning errors can be identified. The diagnostic test attempts to answer such questions as the following: Are the students having difficulty in addition because they don't know certain number combinations or because they don't know how to carry? Are the students' difficulties in reading German due to their inadequate knowledge of vocabulary or to their poor grasp of certain elements of grammar? Are the students unable to apply scientific principles to new situations because they don't understand the principles, because their knowledge of particular concepts is weak, or because the new situations are too unfamiliar to them? Thus, the diagnostic test focuses on the common sources of error encountered by students, so that the learning difficulties can be pinpointed and remedied.

Diagnosing learning problems is a matter of degree. The formative test determines whether a student has mastered the learning tasks being taught and, if not, prescribes how to remedy the learning failures. The diagnostic test is designed to probe deeper into the causes of learning deficiencies that are left unresolved by formative testing. Of course, this is not to imply that all learning problems can be overcome by formative and diagnostic testing. These are simply tools to aid in the identification and diagnosis of specific learning difficulties so that appropriate remedial steps can be taken. Diagnosing and remedying severe learning problems frequently requires a wide array of evaluative tools and the services of specially trained personnel. All we are attempting to do here is to show how formative and diagnostic tests can contribute to improved student learning during instruction. The model presented in Figure 1.2 summarizes the process.

End of Instruction (Summative Testing)

At the end of a course or unit of instruction we are concerned primarily with the extent to which the students have achieved the intended outcomes of the instruction. Questions such as the following must be answered:

1. Which students have mastered the learning tasks to such a degree that they should proceed to the next course or unit of instruction?
2. What grade should be assigned to each student?

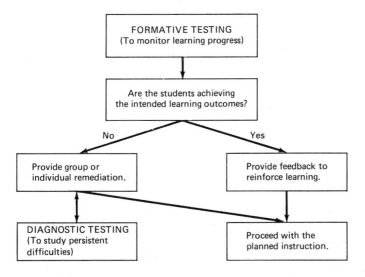

FIGURE 1.2. Simplified Model for the Instructional Role of Formative Testing.

The achievement test given at the end of a period of instruction for the purpose of certifying mastery or assigning grades is called a *summative* test. These tests are tyically broad in coverage and attempt to measure a representative sample of all of the learning tasks included in the instruction. Although the results are used primarily for grading, they can contribute to greater future learning by providing information for evaluating the effectiveness of the instruction. See Figure 1.3 for the summative testing model.

FIGURE 1.3. Simplified Model for the Instructional Role of Summative Testing.

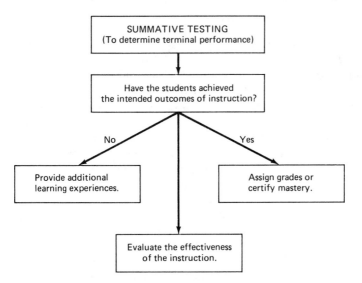

OTHER WAYS TESTS CAN AID LEARNING

As noted in the last section, achievement tests can aid the teacher in making various instructional decisions having a direct influence on student learning. In addition, tests can aid student learning in a number of other ways.

Tests Can Aid Student Motivation

A carefully planned achievement testing program can have a direct influence on student learning by (1) providing them with short-term goals, (2) clarifying the types of tasks to be learned, and (3) providing feedback concerning their learning progress. Short-term goals are more motivating than admonitions that "some day you will find this information useful." An expected test stimulates learning activity and directs it toward the learning tasks to be covered by the test. Although this influence of testing is sometimes considered undesirable, as when the test measures only factual information, it need not be a negative influence. Its contribution to learning depends to a large extent on how faithfully our tests reflect all of the important outcomes of the instruction and how we use the results. For example, if the application of principles is stressed in our testing as well as in our teaching, we can expect students to direct greater efforts toward learning how to apply principles. Also, if the test results are reported to students as soon as possible, this feedback concerning their strengths and weaknesses in the application of principles will further clarify the nature of the task and indicate what changes are needed for effective performance. Thus, properly constructed tests can motivate students to work toward the instructional objectives of a course by arousing greater learning activity, by directing it toward the intended learning outcomes, and by providing prompt knowledge of results.

Tests Can Aid Retention and Transfer of Learning

Because tests tend to direct students' learning efforts toward the intended outcomes of instruction, they can be used as tools for increasing the retention and transfer of learning. In general, learning outcomes at the understanding, application, and interpretation levels are likely to be retained longer and to have greater transfer value than outcomes at the knowledge level. By including measures of these more complex learning outcomes in our tests, we can direct attention to their importance and provide reinforcing practice in the skills, applications, and interpretations we are attempting to develop. Thus, tests can be used to supplement and complement our teaching efforts in these areas and thereby increase the likelihood that the learning will be of greater permanent value to the students.

Tests Can Aid Student Self-Evaluation

All instruction should be directed toward helping individuals better understand themselves so that they can make more intelligent decisions. Periodic testing and feedback of the results can help students gain insight into what they can do well, the misconceptions that need correction, and the degree of skill they have in various areas. Such information provides the students with a more objective basis for evaluating their strengths and weaknesses. Properly constructed tests tend to provide evidence of learning progress in such an objective and impartial way that the results can be accepted with little resistance or distortion. This assumes, of course, that the tests are properly constructed and are being used to improve learning rather than to threaten or label students. In the latter instance, self-evaluation is apt to be distorted by the psychological defense mechanisms an individual uses to maintain a positive self-image.

Tests Can Aid in Evaluating Instructional Effectiveness

Achievement test results can be used to evaluate the effectiveness of various aspects of the instructional process. For example, they can help determine the extent to which the instructional objectives were realistic, whether the methods and materials of instruction were appropriate, and how well the learning experiences were sequenced. When the majority of the students do poorly on the same test items, it may be the fault of the students but the difficulty is more likely to be found in the instruction. The teacher may be striving for learning outcomes that are unattainable by the students, may be using inappropriate materials, or may be using ineffective methods for bringing about the desired changes. An analysis of the students' responses to the test and the post-test discussion of the results should provide clues to the source of the instructional difficulty so that corrective steps can be taken.

MINIMUM COMPETENCY TESTING AND STUDENT LEARNING

One of the most wide-ranging attempts to use tests to improve student learning can be seen in the development of minimum competency testing programs. The majority of states has now mandated some type of state-wide minimum competency testing. These programs typically involve testing in the basic skills (reading, mathematics, and language usage), and in some cases in such areas as citizenship, consumer education, health education, and career planning. The tests frequently serve as a graduation requirement and students must demonstrate a satisfactory level of performance before receiving a high school diploma. Students who fail the tests are typically provided with remedial instruction and retesting. Repeated failure might result in the granting of a certificate of attendance instead of a diploma. In some states, competency tests are also given in the lower grades to monitor learning progress and identify weaknesses that can be remedied early in the students' educational development.

The minimum competency testing movement has focused national attention on the role of tests in improving learning. There is a real danger, however, that (1) the emphasis on *minimum* competency might direct so much effort toward low scoring students that it leads to the neglect of average and high achieving students, and (2) the narrow focus of the competency tests on basic and life skills might result in less attention being given to other intended learning outcomes. These potential hazards can, of course, be partially offset by the use of classroom achievement tests that are carefully designed to measure all important outcomes of the instruction. How to construct such tests is the major focus of this book.

GUIDELINES FOR ACHIEVEMENT TESTING

Achievement tests are likely to make their greatest contribution to improved learning and instruction if test development is guided by a basic set of principles. The following principles provide a general framework for constructing achievement tests that are most effective in the teaching-learning process.

1. Achievement tests should measure clearly defined learning outcomes. The first step in test development is not the writing of test items but rather the clarification of what is to be measured. This includes considerations such as the following:

1. What are the intended learning outcomes to be measured? These are determined by the instructional objectives of the unit or course (e.g., knowledge of terms, knowledge of facts, understanding of concepts, application of principles).
2. What *specific* student responses will provide evidence that the learning outcomes have been achieved (e.g., "Students know terms" when they can (a) define the terms in their own words, (b) use the term in an original sentence, and (c) distinguish between terms that are similar in meaning)?

When the intended learning outcomes are clearly stated in terms of student performance it helps in selecting the types of test items to write. If we expect students to be able to "define terms in their own words," for example, we simply give them the terms and ask them to write definitions. A true-false or multiple-choice item would provide an inappropriate measure of this specific type of student performance.

2. Achievement tests should be concerned with all intended learning outcomes. In specifying the learning outcomes to be measured, attention should be given to all important outcomes. There is a temptation to focus on simple knowledge and skill outcomes because they are so easy to specify and measure. However, it we want to encourage students to go beyond the memorization of factual information, we must also include outcomes in the areas of understanding, application, and other complex types of learning. If we teach for understanding and application but do not test for it, students are not likely to give it much emphasis in their study. Letting students know that the tests will measure all levels of learning is one way that achievement testing can make a direct contribution to improved learning.

3. Achievement tests should measure a representative sample of instructionally relevant learning tasks. Testing is always a matter of sampling. We seldom can ask all of the questions that we would like to ask in a test. Our instruction might cover hundreds of facts, terms, understandings, applications, and skills, but because of the time available for testing and other constraints we can include only enough items to measure a portion of them. It is the responsibility of the test maker to use a systematic procedure for obtaining a representative sample of test items relevant to the instruction. This involves proceeding from the intended outcomes of instruction (what students should be learning) to the domain of achievement for a particular test (what should be measured) and then to the test itself (what sample of test tasks to include). An instructionally relevant test requires that the instruction, the achievement domain, and the achievement test all be in close agreement (see Figure 1.4).

The selection of a representative sample of tasks for an achievement test can be easily illustrated with an example. Let's assume that an achievement domain specifies that students should be able to define 100 technical terms that have been included in the instruction. Because of time restrictions we can include only 20 items in our test. A fairly representative sample of these terms could be obtained, in this case, by simply placing the 100 words in alphabetical order and selecting every fifth word. Such careful sampling would enable us to generalize from the students' performance on the test sample to their probable performance on the larger domain of words that the test represents. Thus, if a student defined 90 percent of the words correctly on the 20-item test, we can assume that he or she probably could also define approximately 90 percent of the 100 words from which the sample was drawn. Since we are always interested in generalizing from the test sample to the larger achievement domain, the representativeness of the test sample is a key element in constructing an effective measure of achievement.

The procedures involved in obtaining a representative sample of tasks for testing purposes are typically much more involved than our simple example. Because achievement tests are commonly designed to measure a variety of learning tasks, more elaborate test specifications are needed. The procedure for preparing test specifications will be described in the following chapter.

FIGURE 1.4.
Sequence in Constructing Instructionally Relevant Tests.

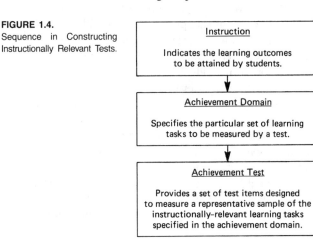

Instruction

Indicates the learning outcomes to be attained by students.

Achievement Domain

Specifies the particular set of learning tasks to be measured by a test.

Achievement Test

Provides a set of test items designed to measure a representative sample of the instructionally-relevant learning tasks specified in the achievement domain.

4. Achievement tests should include the types of test items that are most appropriate for measuring the intended learning outcomes. The learning outcomes for a course or unit of study specify the types of performance we are willing to accept as evidence of student achievement. The achievement test is simply a device for calling forth the specified performance so that judgments can be made concerning the extent to which learning has taken place. The key to effective achievement testing is to select the most appropriate item type and to construct it so carefully that it elicits the desired response.

In some cases a variety of item types may be needed to measure an intended learning outcome. By combining item types we can make up for a weakness in one by using the strength of the other. In determining students' ability to write, for example, logic would tell us that the best procedure is to have them write something. This obviously would provide the most direct measure of writing ability. However, in completing the assignment some students may select only those words they know well and can spell properly and write sentences that need only simple punctuation. Thus, a comprehensive measure of writing skills would require the use of supplementary measures of vocabulary, spelling, and punctuation. Using short-answer tests in these areas makes it possible to obtain systematic coverage of specific writing skills not possible with the writing project. Therefore, it is not a matter of either using a writing project or using short-answer tests. The two supplement and complement each other and the use of both results in more complete information.

5. Achievement tests should be based on plans for using the results. During the process of constructing achievement tests, consideration should be given to how the results will be used. For example, givng a pretest at the beginning of a unit or a course will be of little value unless plans are made to use the results to modify instruction as needed. Similarly, administering a diagnostic test presumes that remedial teaching will follow. In the use of other types of achievement tests (e.g., formative tests), plans for feedback of results to students are needed if the tests are to help students improve their learning.

We are more likely to construct appropriate tests and use them effectively if our intentions for use are given careful consideration when teaching plans are made. In constructing a test to measure learning progress, for example, we may want to key each set of items measuring the same learning task to reference materials so that students can do individual study in remedying their learning errors. Thus, by considering the use of test results during instructional planning, we can maximize the contribution that tests make to the teaching-learning process.

6. Achievement tests should provide scores that are relatively free from measurement errors. A well-constructed achievement test should provide consistent results. If we obtain a set of test scores for our students, we need to be confident that we would get similar scores if we tested them at a different time or with a different, but equivalent, sample of items. Unless our measures provide this kind of generalizability concerning student achievement, little confidence can be placed in a given set of scores. The degree to which test scores provide consistent, and thus reliable, results depends on the extent to which errors of measurement are present.

There are a number of factors that increase the amount of error in test scores. Ambiguous test items will introduce errors into the scores. Testing a specific skill with too few test items will provide scores that are more influenced by chance factors than by student performance. The subjectivity of scoring essay tests will introduce errors into the scores. During testing, variations in the students' attention, effort, fatigue, and tendency to guess will influence the consistency of their test responses and thereby introduce error. Many of the sources of measurement error can be controlled through care in the construction and administration of tests. Where the sources of error cannot be eliminated as in scoring essay questions, they can be taken into account during the interpretation of the results. We can make only tentative interpretations and seek verification from other evidence of achievement.

NORM-REFERENCED AND CRITERION-REFERENCED TESTING

As we noted earlier, an achievement test can be used to provide (1) a relative ranking of students, or (2) a description of the learning tasks a student can and cannot perform. Test results of the first type are interpreted in terms of each student's relative standing among other students (for example, "He is third highest in a class of 35 students"). This method of interpreting test performance is called *norm-referenced* interpretation. Test results of the second type are expressed in terms of the specific knowledge and skills each student can demonstrate (for instance, "He can identify all parts of the microscope and demonstrate its proper use"). This method of interpreting test results is called *criterion-referenced* interpretation. Both methods of describing test results are useful. The first tells how an individual's test performance compares with that of others. The second tells in specific performance terms what an individual can do without reference to the performance of others.

Strictly speaking, the terms *norm referenced* and *criterion referenced* refer only to the method of interpreting test results. Thus, both types of interpretation could be applied to the same test. For example, we might say, "Joan surpassed 90 percent of the students (norm-referenced interpretation) by correctly completing 20 of the 25 chemical equations" (criterion-referenced interpretation). The two types of test interpretation are likely to be most meaningful, however, when the test is designed specifically for the type of interpretation to be made. In general, norm-referenced interpretation is facilitated by tests that provide a wide spread of scores so that reliable discriminations can be made among students at various levels of achievement. This is typically done by eliminating easy test items and favoring items of average difficulty. On the other hand, criterion-referenced interpretation is facilitated by including test items that are directly relevant to the learning outcomes, whether or not they are easy for students. Eliminating the easy items would provide incomplete descriptions of student performances because such descriptions would not include those learning tasks that were mastered by *all* students. Since each type of interpretation is favored by a different approach to test construction, the terms *norm-referenced test* and *criterion-referenced test* have come into widespread use.

A summary of some common characteristics of tests that are specifically designed to emphasize each type of interpretation is presented in Table 1.1. It must be kept in mind, however, that these are primarily matters of emphasis. For example, norm-referenced tests are typically, but not exclusively, used for surveying achievement over a wide range of learning outcomes. By the same token criterion-referenced tests are typically, but not exclusively, used for mastery testing. A review of the characteristics of each testing approach in Table 1.1 will reveal the differences that exist when each test is constructed to serve its principal use.

TABLE 1.1   Summary Comparison of Two Basic Approaches to Achievement Testing

	NORM-REFERENCED TESTING	CRITERION-REFERENCED TESTING
Principal Use	Survey testing.	Mastery testing.
Major Emphasis	Measure individual differences in achievement.	Describe tasks students can perform.
Interpretation of Results	Compare performance to that of other individuals.	Compare performance to a clearly specified achievement domain.
Content Coverage	Typically covers a broad area of achievement.	Typically focuses on a limited set of learning tasks.
Nature of Test Plan	Table of specifications is commonly used.	Detailed domain specifications are favored.
Item Selection Procedures	Items are selected that provide maximum discrimination among individuals (to obtain high score variability). Easy items are typically eliminated from the test.	Includes all items needed to adequately describe performance. No attempt is made to alter item difficulty or to eliminate easy items to increase score variability.
Performance Standards	Level of performance is determined by *relative* position in some known group (ranks fifth in a group of twenty).	Level of performance is commonly determined by *absolute* standards (demonstrates mastery by defining 90 percent of the technical terms).

Constructing Norm-Referenced and Criterion-Referenced Tests

There are more similarities than differences in the preparation of norm-referenced tests (NRT) and criterion-referenced tests (CRT), and, as noted earlier, the differences are largely a matter of emphasis. The following statements highlight some of the major similarities and differences in constructing NRTs and CRTs for measuring achievement.

1. Both typically require specification of the intended learning outcomes as a basis for test construction.

    NRT—The intended learning outcomes may be described in general or specific terms.

    CRT—The intended learning outcomes tend to be described in specific terms.

2. Both are typically designed to measure a representative sample of the specified learning outcomes.

    NRT—Usually covers a broad range of outcomes with few test items per outcome.

    CRT —Usually covers a delimited domain of outcomes with numerous test items per outcome.

3. Both use a variety of types of test items.

    NRT—Selection-type items (e.g., multiple choice) are highly favored.

    CRT —There is somewhat less dependence on selection-type items.

4. Both require the application of a common set of item-writing rules.

    NRT—The ability of items to *discriminate* among students is emphasized.

    CRT —The ability of items to *describe* student performance on specific learning tasks is emphasized.

5. Both require attention to the reliability of the results.

    NRT—The traditional statistical procedures for estimating reliability are appropriate because of high score variability.

    CRT —The traditional statistical procedures for estimating reliability are inappropriate due to limited score variability (see Chapter 9).

6. Both require care in interpreting the results.

    NRT—Knowing the nature of the group is especially important in evaluating a student's relative standing.

    CRT —Knowing the nature of the achievement domain is especially important in describing a student's performance.

These two test types are probably best viewed as the ends of a continuum rather than as discrete categories. Many test publishers have combined the best features of each by making norm-referenced tests more descriptive (e.g., by combining items into meaningful item clusters for C-R interpretation) and by adding norm-referenced interpretation to criterion-referenced tests. This use of dual interpretation requires compromises in test construction and caution in use of the test scores, but the increased information concerning student achievement contributes to the usefulness of the test results.

Most of the discussions of test construction in the following chapters will apply to both test types. Where there are significant differences in test development procedures, these will be noted.

SUMMARY OF POINTS

The emphasis in this chapter can be summarized by the following points.

1. The main purpose of achievement testing is to improve student learning.

2. Achievement tests can be used for measuring entry performance (placement

tests), monitoring learning progress (formative and diagnostic tests), or measuring end-of-instruction achievement (summative tests).

3. Achievement tests can contribute to student motivation, the retention and transfer of learning, student self-evaluation skills, and an evaluation of instructional effectiveness.

4. Minimum competency testing is a nationwide attempt to use tests to improve student learning.

5. The first step in achievement testing is to clearly specify the domain of achievement to be measured.

6. Achievement tests should be designed to measure a representative sample of the instructionally relevant learning tasks specified in the achievement domain.

7. The types of items used in an achievement test should be determined primarily by the learning tasks to be measured.

8. Achievement tests should provide dependable scores that are in harmony with their intended use.

9. Achievement tests can be interpreted by comparing a student's performance to that of others (norm referenced) or by describing the student's performance on a clearly defined set of tasks (criterion referenced).

10. Norm-referenced and criterion-referenced tests are best viewed as the ends of a continuum rather than as discrete categories.

11. Tests can be developed that emphasize norm-referenced interpretation (e.g., survey tests), criterion-referenced interpretation (e.g., mastery tests), or a combination of the two.

12. Dual interpretation requires compromises in test construction and caution in test interpretation but it provides increased information concerning an individual's achievement.

ADDITIONAL READING

BERK, R. A., ED., *A Guide to Criterion–Referenced Test Construction* (Baltimore, Maryland: Johns Hopkins University Press, 1984). See Chapter 1 by A. J. Nitko, "Defining 'Criterion-Referenced Test' " for a review of the many definitions of criterion referencing.

BLOOM, B. S., MADAUS, G. T., AND J. T. HASTINGS, *Evaluation to Improve Learning* (New York: McGraw-Hill, 1981). See Chapters 4, 5, and 6. Provides a comprehensive treatment of summative, diagnostic, and formative evaluation.

GRONLUND, N. E., *Measurement and Evaluation in Teaching*, 5th ed. (New York: Macmillan Publishing Co., Inc., 1985). See Chapter 1. Presents the principles and procedures of classroom testing and its role in the instrucitonal process.

POPHAM, W. J. *Modern Educational Measurement* (Englewood Cliffs, N.J.: Prentice-Hall, Inc., 1981). See Chapter 2, "Norm-Referenced and Criterion-Referenced Measurement," for a comparison of the two types and examples of educational decisions where each is more useful.

TITLE, C. K., "COMPETENCY TESTING." In *Encyclopedia of Educational Research*, 5th ed. (New York: Macmillan Publishing Co., Inc., 1982), Vol. 1, pp. 333-352. Describes minimum competency testing and the measurement, policy, and legal issues involved.

2

Planning the Test

The key to effective achievement testing is careful planning. It provides greater assurance that our test will measure relevant learning outcomes . . . measure a representative sample of the desired outcomes . . . and provide dependable information on which to base instructional decisions. . . . Test planning involves the identification and specification of precisely what is to be measured.

The planning of an achievement test can take many forms, both professional test makers and classroom teachers have found the following series of steps to be most useful.

1. Determine the purpose of the test.
2. Identify and define the intended learning outcomes.
3. Prepare the test specifications.
4. Construct relevant test items.

It is obvious from these steps that the first consideration in test planning is to determine the type of test to be prepared. This will help clarify what is to be measured and will aid in stating the test specifications in such precise terms that test items can be constructed to call forth the desired performance. If the test planning is carefully done, constructing relevant test items is greatly simplified.

DETERMINING THE PURPOSE OF THE TEST

As we noted in Chapter 1, tests can be used in an instructional program to assess entry behavior (placement test), monitor learning progress (formative test), diagnose learning difficulties (diagnostic test), and measure performance at the end of instruction (summative test). Each type of test use typically requires some modification in test design. Although the specific makeup of any test depends on the particular situation in which it is to be used, it is possible to identify common characteristics of the various test types. These have been summarized in Table 2.1.

TABLE 2.1   Characteristics of Four Types of Achievement Tests

TYPE OF TEST	FUNCTION OF TEST	SAMPLING CONSIDERATIONS	ITEM CHARACTERISTICS
	Measure prerequisite entry skills	Include each prerequisite entry behavior	Typically, items are easy and criterion-referenced
Placement	Determine entry performance on course objectives	Select representative sample of course objectives	Typically, items have a wide range of difficulty and are norm referenced
Formative	Provide feedback to students and teacher on learning progress	Include all unit objectives if possible (or those most essential)	Items match difficulty of unit objectives and are criterion referenced
Diagnostic	Determine causes of recurring learning difficulties	Include sample of tasks based on common sources of learning error	Typically, items are easy and are used to pinpoint specific causes of error
Summative	Assign grades, or certify mastery, at end of instruction	Select representative sample of course objectives	Typically, items have a wide range of difficulty and are norm referenced

Adapted from P. W. Airasian and G. F. Madaus, "Functional Types of Student Evaluation," *Measurement and Evaluation in Guidance*, 4 (1972), 221-33.

The material in Table 2.1 provides a good general description of the four basic test types we have discussed, but it must be recognized that the categories overlap to some degree. In some instances, a particular test may be designed to serve more than one function. For example, an end-of-unit formative test may be used to provide feedback to students, to pinpoint sources of learning error, and to certify mastery of unit objectives. Similarly, sampling considerations and item characteristics may need to be modified to fit a particular test use or a specific type of instruction. Despite the lack of discrete categories, however, the table highlights the variety of functions that achievement tests can serve and the basic framework for planning achievement tests that are designed to be of maximum usefulness.

IDENTIFYING AND DEFINING
THE INTENDED LEARNING OUTCOMES

The learning outcomes measured by a test should faithfully reflect the objectives of instruction. Thus, the first order of business is to identify those instructional objectives that are to be measured by the test and then make certain that they are stated in a manner that is useful for testing. This is easier said than done. It is especially difficult if a clearly defined set of instructional objectives is not available to begin with, as is usually the case. One useful guide for approaching this task is the *Taxonomy of Educational Objectives* (see Bloom and others, 1956). This is a comprehensive system that classifies objectives within each of three domains: (1) cognitive, (2) affective, and (3) psychomotor. The cognitive domain of the taxonomy is concerned with intellectual outcomes, the affective domain with interests and attitudes, and the psychomotor domain with motor skills (see Gronlund, 1985, for a summary of each). Since our concern here is with achievement testing, we shall focus primarily on the cognitive domain.

Cognitive Domain of the Taxonomy

Intellectual outcomes in the cognitive domain are divided into two major classes: (1) knowledge and (2) intellectual abilities and skills. These are further subdivided into six main areas as follows:

KNOWLEDGE

1.00 KNOWLEDGE (Remembering previously learned material)
    1.10 Knowledge of specifics
      1.11 Knowledge of terms
      1.12 Knowledge of specific facts
      1.20 Knowledge of ways and means of dealing with specifics
      1.21 Knowledge of conventions
      1.22 Knowledge of trends and sequences
      1.23 Knowledge of classifications and categories
      1.24 Knowledge of criteria
      1.25 Knowledge of methodology
      1.30 Knowledge of the universals and abstractions in a field
      1.31 Knowledge of principles and generalizations
      1.32 Knowledge of theories and structures

INTELLECTUAL ABILITIES AND SKILLS

2.00 COMPREHENSION (Grasping the meaning of material)
    2.10 Translation (Converting from one form to another)
    2.20 Interpretation (Explaining or summarizing material)
    2.30 Extrapolation (Extending the meaning beyond the data)
3.00 APPLICATION (Using information in concrete situations)
4.00 ANALYSIS (Breaking down material into its parts)
    4.10 Analysis of elements (Identifying the parts)
    4.20 Analysis of relationships (Identifying the relationship)
    4.30 Analysis of organizational principles (Identifying the organization)
5.00 SYNTHESIS (Putting parts together into a whole)
    5.10 Production of a unique communication
    5.20 Production of a plan or proposed set of operations
    5.30 Derivation of a set of abstract relations
    6.00 EVALUATION (Judging the value of a thing for a given purpose using definite criteria)

6.10 Judgments in terms of internal evidence
6.20 Judgments in terms of external criteria[1]

As can be seen in this outline the outcomes are arranged in order of increasing complexity. They begin with the relatively simple recall of factual information, proceed to the lowest level of understanding (comprehension), and then advance through the increasingly complex levels of application, analysis, synthesis, and evaluation. The subdivisions within each area are also listed in order of increasing complexity. This scheme for classifying student behavior is thus hierarchical; that is, the more complex behaviors include the simpler behaviors listed in the lower categories.

The cognitive domain of the taxonomy is especially useful in planning the achievement test. It focuses on a comprehensive and apparently complete list of mental processes to be considered when identifying learning outcomes, it provides a standard vocabulary for describing and classifying learning outcomes, and it serves as a guide for stating learning outcomes in terms of specific student performance.

Although the cognitive domain of the taxonomy provides a valuable guide for identifying learning outcomes, not all of the areas listed under this domain will be covered in a particular test or even in a particular course. Moreover, the classification scheme is neutral concerning the relative importance of the learning outcomes listed. Thus, it is the instructor who must decide which learning outcomes will guide their teaching and testing, and how much emphasis each outcome will receive. The taxonomy serves merely as a convenient checklist of outcomes that prevents relevant areas of student performance from being overlooked during the planning of an achievement test.

Stating the General Learning Outcomes

The learning outcomes to be measured by a test are most useful in test construction when they are stated as *terminal performance* that is *observable*. That is, they should clearly indicate the student performance to be demonstrated at the end of the learning experience. The following list of learning outcomes for a unit in the planning of an achievement test illustrates this type of statement. It should be noted that these statements include only objectives that can be tested and that they are stated as *general outcomes*. Before being used for test construction, each one would need to be further defined in terms of specific learning outcomes.

At the end of this unit in achievement test planning the student will demonstrate that he or she:

1. Knows the meaning of common terms.
2. Knows specific facts about test planning.
3. Knows the basic procedures for planning an achievement test.

---

[1]Reprinted from Benjamin S. Bloom, ed., and others, *Taxonomy of Educational Objectives: Cognitive Domain* (New York: David McKay Co., Inc., 1956), pp. 201-207. Reprinted with permission of the publisher.

4. Comprehends the relevant principles of testing.
5. Applies the principles in test planning.

These statements of general learning outcomes have been deliberately kept free of specific course content so that with only slight modification they can be used with various units of study. As we shall see later, the test specifications provide a means of relating intended outcomes to specific subject matter topics.

This list of general outcomes could, of course, be expanded by making the statements more specific, and in some cases it may be desirable to do so. The number of general learning outcomes to use is somewhat arbitrary, but somewhere between five and fifteen provide a list that is both useful and manageable. Typically, a shorter list is satisfactory for a unit of study, while a more comprehensive list is needed for summative testing at the end of a course.

Defining the General Outcomes in Specific Terms

When a satisfactory list of general learning outcomes has been identified and clearly stated, the next step is to list the specific types of student performance that are to be accepted as evidence that the outcomes have been achieved. For example, what specific types of performance will show that a student "knows the meaning of common terms" or "comprehends the relevant principle of testing"? For these two areas the specific learning outcomes may be listed a follows:

1. Knows the meaning of common terms.
   1.1 Identifies the correct definitions of terms.
   1.2 Identifies the meaning of terms when used in context.
   1.3 Distinguishes between terms on basis of meaning.
   1.4 Selects the most appropriate terms when describing testing procedures.

4. Comprehends the relevant principles of testing.
   4.1 Decribes each principle in his or her own words.
   4.2 Matches a specific example to each principle.
   4.3 Explains the relevance of each principle to the major steps in test planning.
   4.4 Predicts the most probable effect of violating each of the principles.
   4.5 Formulates a test plan that is in harmony with the principles.

Note that the terms used to describe the specific learning outcomes indicate student performance that can be demonstrated to an outside observer. That is, they are *observable* responses that can be called forth by test items. The key terms are listed below to emphasize what is meant by defining learning outcomes in *specific performance terms*.

Identifies	Matches
Distinguishes between	Explains
Selects	Predicts
Describes	Formulates

Action verbs such as these indicate precisely what the student is able to do to demonstrate achievement. Such vague and indefinite terms as "learns," "sees," "realizes," and "is familiar with" should be avoided, since they do not clearly indicate the terminal performance to be measured.

Sample action verbs for stating specific learning outcomes at each level of the cognitive domain of the taxonomy are presented in Table 2.2. Although certain action verbs may be used at several different levels (e.g., "identifies"), the table provides a useful guide for defining intended outcomes in performance terms. For more comprehensive lists of action verbs, see the references by Gronlund (1985, 1985) listed at the end of this chapter.

In defining the general learning outcomes in specific performance terms, it is typically impossible to list all of the relevant types of performance. The proportion that need be listed depends to a large extent on the nature of the test. In planning a test that is to be used to *describe* which learning tasks a student has mastered (criterion-referenced test), we should like as comprehensive a list as possible. For a test that is used to *rank* students in order of achievement (norm-referenced test), however, it is usually satisfactory to include a sufficient number of specific types of performance to clarify what the typical student is like who has achieved the intended outcomes.

TABLE 2.2   Illustrative Action Verbs for Defining Objectives in the Cognitive Domain of the Taxonomy

TAXONOMY CATEGORIES	SAMPLE VERBS FOR STATING SPECIFIC LEARNING OUTCOMES
Knowledge	Identifies, names, defines, describes, lists, matches, selects, outlines
Comprehension	Classifies, explains, summarizes, converts, predicts, distinguishes between
Application	Demonstrates, computes, solves, modifies, arranges, operates, relates
Analysis	Differentiaties, diagrams, estimates, separates, infers, orders, subdivides
Synthesis	Combines, creates, formulates, designs, composes, constructs, rearranges, revises
Evaluation	Judges, criticizes, compares, justifies, concludes, discriminates, supports

PREPARING THE TEST SPECIFICATIONS

The writing of test items should be guided by a carefully prepared set of test specifications. The function of the specifications is to describe the achievement domain being measured and to provide guidelines for obtaining a respresentative sample of test tasks. Although the nature and detail of test specifications can be expected to vary considerably, here we shall describe two of the more commonly recommended procedures. In the construction of norm-referenced achievement tests, one of the most widely used devices has been a two-way chart called a *table of specifications*.

Building a Table of Specifications

Preparing a table of specifications involves (1) selecting the learning outcomes to be tested, (2) outlining the subject matter, and (3) making a two-way chart. The two-way chart describes the sample of items to be included in the test.

Selecting the Learning Outcomes to be Tested.   The learning outcomes for a particular course will depend on the specific nature of the course, the objectives attained in previous courses, the philosophy of the school, the special needs of the students, and a host of other local factors that have a bearing on the instructional program. Despite the variation from course to course, most lists of instructional objectives will include learning outcomes in the following areas: (1) knowledge, (2) intellectual abilities and skills, (3) general skills (laboratory, performance, communication, work-study), and (4) attitudes, interests and appreciations. It is in the first two areas covered by the cognitive domain of the taxonomy that achievement testing is most useful. Learning outcomes in the other areas are typically evaluated by rating scales, checklists, anecdotal records, inventories, and similar nontest evaluation procedures. Thus, the first step is to separate from the list of learning outcomes those that are testable by paper-and-pencil test. The selected list of learning outcomes should, of course, be defined in specific terms, as described in the previous section. Clarifying the specific types of performance to be called forth by the test will aid in constructing test terms that are most relevant to the intended learning outcomes.

Outlining the Subject Matter.   The stated learning outcomes specify how students are expected to react to the subject matter of a course. Although it is possible to include both the student performance and the specific subject matter the student is to react toward in the same statement, it is usually desirable to list them separately. The reason for this is that the student can react in the same way to many different areas of subject matter, and he or she can react in many different ways to the same area of subject matter. For example, when we state that a student can "define a term in his or her own words," "recall a specific fact," or "identify an example of a principle," these types of performance can be applied to almost any area of subject matter. Similarly, in studying the taxonomy of educational objectives we may expect students merely to recall the categories in it, or we could require them to explain the principles on which it is organized, to summarize its usefulness in test planning, to classify a given set of learning outcomes with it, or to use it in the actual construction of a test. Since particular types of student performance can overlap a variety of subject matter areas, and vice versa, it is more convenient to list each aspect of performance and subject matter separately and then to relate them in the table of specifications.

The content of a course may be outlined in detail for teaching purposes, but for test planning only the major categories need be listed. The following outline of subject matter topics covered in the first two chapters of this book illustrates sufficient detail for the test plan.

A. Role of testing in the instructional process
     1. Instructional decisions and test types
     2. Influence of tests on learning and instruction
B. Principles of achievement testing
     1. Relation to instructional objectives
     2. Representative sampling
     3. Relevance of items to outcomes
     4. Relevance of test to use of results
     5. Reliability of results
     6. Improvement of learning
C. Norm-referenced versus criterion-referenced testing
D. Planning the test
     1. Determining the purpose of the test
     2. Identifying the intended learning outcomes
     3. Preparing the test specifications
     4. Constructing relevant test items

In using the topics in this book for illustrative purposes, there is no implication that the content outline should be limited to the material in a particular book. An achievement test is typically designed to measure all of the course content, including that covered in class discussion, outside reading, and other special assignments. Our example here is meant to illustrate the approximate amount of detail and not the source of the topics to be included.

Making the Two-Way Chart.   When the learning outcomes have been selected and clearly defined and the course content outlined, the two-way chart should be prepared. This is called a table of specifications. It relates outcomes to content and indicates the relative weight to be given to each of the various areas. As noted earlier, the purpose of the table is to provide assurance that the test will measure a representative sample of the learning outcomes and the subject matter topics to be measured.

An example of a table of specifications for a norm-referenced summative test on the first two chapters of this book is given in Table 2.3. Note that only the general learning outcomes relevant to these chapters and only the major subject matter categories have been included. A more detailed table may be desirable for test purposes, but this is sufficient for illustration.

The numbers in each cell of the table indicate the number of test items to be devoted to that area. For example, 15 items in the test will measure knowledge of terms; four of them pertain to the ''role of tests'' in instruction,'' four to ''principles of testing,'' four to ''norm referenced versus criterion referenced,'' and three to ''planning the test.'' The number of items assigned to each cell is determined by the weight given to each learning outcome and each subject matter area.

A number of factors will enter into assigning relative weights to each learning outcome and each content area. How important is each area in the total learning experience? How much time was devoted to each area during instruction? Which outcomes have the greater retention and transfer value? What relative importance do curriculum specialists assign to each area? These and similar criteria must be con-

TABLE 2.3 Table of Specifications for a Summative Test on Chapters 1 and 2 of This Book

OUTCOMES / CONTENT	KNOWS			COMPREHENDS PRINCIPLES	APPLIES PRINCIPLES	TOTAL NUMBER OF ITEMS
	TERMS	FACTS	PROCEDURES			
Role of Tests in Instruction	4	4		2		10
Principles of Testing	4	3	2	6	5	20
Norm Referenced versus Criterion Referenced	4	3	3			10
Planning the Test	3	5	5	2	5	20
Total Number of Items	15	15	10	10	10	60

sidered. In the final analysis, however, the weights assigned in the table should faithfully reflect the emphasis given during instruction. In Table 2.3, for example, it is assumed that twice as much emphasis was given to "planning the test" (20 items) as was given to "norm referenced versus criterion referenced" (10 items). Similarly, it is assumed that knowledge outcomes were given approximately two-thirds of the emphasis during instruction (40 items) and that comprehension and application outcomes were each given approximately one-sixth of the total emphasis (10 items each).

In summary, preparing a table of specifications includes the following steps:

1. Identify the learning outcomes and content areas to be measured by the test.
2. Weigh the learning outcomes and content areas in terms of their relative importance.
3. Build the table in accordance with these relative weights by distributing the test items proportionately among the relevant cells of the table.

The resulting two-way table indicates the type of test needed to measure the learning outcomes and course content in a balanced manner. Thus, the table of specifications serves the test maker like a blueprint. It specifies the number and the nature of the items in the test, and it thereby provides a guide for item writing.

Specifications for Criterion-Referenced Tests

Whether a table of specifications is useful in preparing a criterion-referenced test depends greatly on the nature of the achievement domain being measured. In some cases the test may cover such a limited area that a table of specifications is unnecessary. In constructing a test to measure "knowledge of the categories in the cognitive domain of the taxonomy," for example, a list of specific ways students are to demonstrate their knowledge may provide a sufficient basis for test planning. The specifications could then simply indicate the number of items to be used to measure each specific type of performance as shown in Table 2.4. For some pur-

TABLE 2.4   Specific Knowledge Outcomes to Result from Study of the Cognitive Domain of the *Taxonomy* and the Number of Test Items for Each Intended Outcome

TYPES OF STUDENT PERFORMANCE	NUMBER OF ITEMS
Describes the meaning of each major category.	6
Identifies the hierarchical order of the major categories.	4
Identifies a verb that best fits each main category.	6
States a specific learning outcome for each main subcategory.	10
Distinguishes between given pairs of categories.	4

poses it may be desirable to use a listing like that in Table 2.4 *and* a table of specifications. In any event the test plan should indicate the achievement domain to be measured and the specific nature of the student performance to be accepted as evidence of achievement.

When criterion-referenced tests are being prepared by more than one person (e.g., for a mastery testing program) more detailed test specifications are desirable. These specifications should include a description of the test items to be used plus a sample item that illustrates the item characteristics. A brief example of such specifications is shown in Figure 2.1.

An even more comprehensive and detailed set of specifications for criterion-referenced tests has been recommended by Popham (1978, 1984). He suggests writing separate test specifications for each set of items that measure the same class of student performance. This typically involves a clearly defined and delimited achievement domain and includes the following test specification components:[2]

1. *General description:* A brief description, in general terms, of the behavior being assessed by the test.

2. *Sample item:* An illustrative item that reflects the test item attributes to be delimited in the following two components.

3. *Stimulus attributes:* A series of statements that attempt to delimit the class of stimulus material that will be encountered by the examinee.

4. *Response attributes:* A series of statements that attempts either to (a) delimit the class of response or response options from which the student makes *selected responses* or (b) explicate the standards by which an examinee's *constructed responses* will be judged.

5. *Specification supplement:* In certain cases it may be necessary to add an appendix or supplement to the preceding four components. This supplement typically provides a more detailed listing or explanation of eligible content.

FIGURE 2.1.   Specifications for a Ten-Item Test Measuring One Specific Comprehension Outcome.

General Outcome:	Comprehends the meaning of measurement terms.
Specific Outcome:	Identifies an example of each term.
Type of Test:	Multiple choice (10 items).
Item Characteristics:	Each test item will consist of a question or incomplete statement followed by four possible answers placed in alphabetical order. The *correct* answer will be an example that best fits the meaning of the term. The *incorrect* alternatives (distracters) will be made plausible by using common student misunderstandings and by matching the correct answer in terms of length, content, and grammatical structure.
Sample Item:	Which of the following is an example of a *performance term*?
	*A Defines
	B Fears
	C Realizes
	D Thinks

[2]W. J. Popham, *Criterion-Referenced Measurement* (Englewood Cliffs, N.J.: Prentice-Hall, Inc., 1978), pp. 121-122.

Such detailed specifications may run several pages and thus be time consuming to prepare (see Popham, 1978, 1984, for examples). If carefully done, however, the specifications will clearly indicate the nature of the student performance being measured and the specific characteristics of the test items to be prepared. This procedure is especially useful where pools of test items are being prepared for school-wide use and for storage in computer item banks. In this case, the specifications provide the needed guidelines for preparing pools of instructionally relevant and functionally similar test items. The detailed descriptions are, of course, also useful in communicating to the test user specifically what the test measured and, thus, what the test scores represent. Because criterion-referenced tests are designed to describe the tasks that students can perform, detailed specifications are needed for proper interpretation.

CONSIDERATIONS IN CONSTRUCTING
RELEVANT TEST ITEMS

The construction of a set of relevant test items is greatly simplified if the intended learning outcomes have been clearly defined and the test specifications carefully prepared. The quality of the test will then depend on how closely the test maker can match the specifications. Here we shall confine our discussion to some of the general specifications in preparing test items. More detailed procedures and rules for item writing will be described in the chapters that follow.

Selecting the Types of Test Items to Use

The items used in achievement tests can be classified as either *selection-type* items or *supply-type* items. The selection-type item presents students with a set of possible responses from which they are to select the most appropriate answer. The supply-type item requires students to create and supply their own answers. These two major categories can be used to classify the most widely used item types as follows.

SELECTION-TYPE ITEMS

1. Multiple choice
2. True-false
3. Matching
4. Interpretive exercise

SUPPLY-TYPE ITEMS

1. Short-answer
2. Essay (Restricted response)
3. Essay (Extended response)

These categories are sometimes referred to as *recognition* and *recall* items. This is a case of mislabeling that confuses the method of responding with the mental reaction needed to make the response. When measuring knowledge of facts, test responses might be limited to either the recognition or recall of the answer. However, when measuring complex learning outcomes with selection-type items, the answer is not achieved through mere recognition of a previously learned answer. It typically involves some use of higher mental processes to arrive at a solution (e.g., verbal or mathematical reasoning) before the correct answer can be selected. Similarly, a short-answer item may require reasoning or problem solving rather than simply recalling and supplying factual information. Essay answers, of course, typically require analysis, synthesis, and evaluation skills in addition to recall. Using the *selection* and *supply* labels makes clear how the responses are made but it does not imply limits on the types of learning outcomes that can be measured with each.

In deciding which item types to use in a test, a guiding principle should be: *Use the item types that provide the most direct measures of student performance specified by the intended learning outcome.* Thus, if you want to determine if students can spell, have them spell from dictation. If you want to determine if students can solve mathematics problems, have them solve problems and supply the answers. If you want to determine if students can write, have them write something. Use selection-type items for supply-type outcomes only if there is a compelling reason for doing so (e.g., electronic scoring) and then take into account, during interpretation of the results, that a less direct measure has been used. In some cases, of course, both types of items are useful in the same area. For example, a writing project may provide the best evidence of writing skill but a selection-type test would provide the most systematic coverage of the elements of grammar needed for effective writing.

There are a number of achievement areas where either selection-type items or supply-type items would measure equally well. In these cases, our choice between them must be based on other item characteristics. The preparation of good selection-type items is difficult and students can get a proportion of answers correct by guessing. However, these disadvantages are offset by the fact that (1) they can be scored quickly and objectively (i.e., scorers agree on the answers), (2) they eliminate bluffing, (3) they eliminate the influence of writing skill, (4) they provide an extensive sample of student performance (because of the large number of items used), and (5) they provide for the identification of specific learning errors. In comparison, supply-type items are easier to construct (although harder than commonly believed) but more difficult to score. The scoring of short-answer items is contaminated by answers of varying degrees of correctness and by adjustments needed for misspellings. The scoring of essay tests is tedious, time consuming and influenced by bluffing, writing skill, and the shifting of standards during scoring. Another major shortcoming of supply-type items is the limited sample of learning tasks that can be measured. The short-answer item is restricted primarily to measuring knowledge outcomes. Although the essay test is especially suited to measuring complex learning outcomes, its sampling is limited by the relatively few questions that can be included in a test.

A summary comparison of the relative merits of selection-type and supply-type items is presented in Table. 2.5.

TABLE 2.5   Summary of the Relative Merits of Selection-Type Items and Supply-Type Items

CHARACTERISTIC	SELECTION-TYPE ITEMS	SUPPLY-TYPE ITEMS: SHORT-ANSWER	ESSAY
Measures factual information	Yes	Yes	Yes(*)
Measures understanding	Yes	No(**)	Yes
Measures synthesis	No(**)	No(**)	Yes
Easy to construct	No	Yes	Yes
Samples broadly	Yes	Yes	No
Eliminates bluffing	Yes	No	No
Eliminates writing skill	Yes	No	No
Eliminates blind guessing	No	Yes	Yes
Easy to score	Yes	No	No
Scoring is objective	Yes	No	No
Pinpoints learning errors	Yes	Yes	No
Encourages originality	No	No	Yes

(*)The essay test can measure knowledge of facts, but because of scoring and sampling problems it probably should not be used for this purpose.

(**)These items can be designed to measure limited aspects of these characteristics.

Although this should serve as a guide in selecting the types of items to use in a given test, as noted earlier, the most important question to ask is: *Does this item type provide the most direct measure of the intended learning outcome?* If the various item types are equal in this regard, the selection-type items would be favored because of the broad sampling, the objective scoring, and the pinpointing of specific learning errors.

Matching Items to Specific Learning Outcomes

Effective achievement testing requires that a set of test items be constructed that calls forth the performance described in the intended learning outcomes. While we can never be certain of a perfect correspondence between outcome and item, the following examples illustrate how items should be written to measure the specific type of performance stated in the specific learning outcome.

EXAMPLES

Specific Learning Outcome: Defines terms in student's own words.
  Directions: Define each of the following terms in a sentence or two.
    1. Taxonomy
    2. Cognitive
    3. Measurement
    2. Evaluation

Specific Learning Outcome: Identifies procedural steps in planning for a test.
    1. Which one of the following steps should be completed first in planning for an achievement test?[3]

[3]The correct answer is indicated throughout this book by an asterisk.

    A.   Select the types of test items to use.
    B.   Decide on the length of the test.
 *C.   Define the intended learning outcomes.
    D.   Prepare the test specifications.

Specific Learning Outcome: Identifies the hierarchical order of the categories in the cognitive domain of the taxonomy.

   1.   Which one of the following categories in the taxonomy indicates the highest level of learning?
      A.   Analysis
      B.   Application
      C.   Comprehension
    *D.   Synthesis

Specific Learning Outcome: Distinguishes between sound and unsound principles of achievement testing.

Directions: Read each of the following statements. If the statement indicates a sound principle of achievement testing, circle the S; if it indicates an unsound principle, circle the U.

*S   U   1.   The specific learning outcomes to be tested should be stated in terms of student performance.

S *U   2.   Achievement testing should be limited to outcomes that can be measured objectively.

*S   U   3.   Each achievement test item should measure a clearly defined type of student performance.

Specific Learning Outcome: Identifies examples of properly stated learning outcomes.

   1.   Which one of the following learning outcomes is properly stated in performance terms?
      A.   Student realizes the importance of tests in teaching.
      B.   Student has acquired the basic principles of achievement testing.
      C.   Student demonstrates a desire for more experience in test construction.
    *D.   Student predicts the most probable effect of violating a test construction principle.

It should be noted in these examples that each specific learning outcome provides a precise definition of the student performance to be measured, and the test item simply provides a task that makes measurement of the specified performance possible.

Improving the Functioning Content of Items

If test items are to call forth the performance described in the intended learning outcomes, great care must be taken in phrasing the items. We need to eliminate all barriers that might prevent a knowledgeable person from responding and all clues that might lead the uninformed to the correct answer. Only those who have achieved the outcome being measured should get the item right. All others (no matter how intelligent) should miss it.

Some of the common *barriers* to be avoided during test preparation are:

Vocabulary that is unnecessarily difficult.
Sentence structure that is unnecessarily complex.
Statements containing ambiguity.
Statements that are excessively wordy.
Unclear pictorial materials.
Directions that are vague.
Material reflecting race, ethnic, or sex bias.

Awareness of such barriers during the planning and preparation of the test is the first step in their elimination. Essentially we can avoid these barriers by (1) writing each test item so that it presents a clearly formulated task, (2) stating the items in simple, clear language, (3) keeping the items free from biased and nonfunctional material, and (4) using a test format and directions that contribute to effective test taking. Much of the material presented later in this book is directed toward constructing tests that prevent extraneous factors from distorting the test results.

Some of the common *clues* to be avoided during test preparation are:

Verbal associations that give away the answer.
Grammatical inconsistencies that eliminate wrong answers.
Specific determiners that make certain answers probable (e.g., sometimes) and others improbable (e.g., always).
Stereotyped or textbook phrasing of correct answers.
Length or location of correct answers.
Material in an item that aids in answering another item.

Just as in controlling extraneous factors that provide barriers to the correct answer, clues such as these can be eliminated by being aware of them and by following sound principles of test construction. Many of the rules for item writing and test preparation in the chapters that follow provide guidelines for this purpose.

Selecting the Proper Item Difficulty

Decisions concerning item difficulty are guided to a large extent by the nature of the achievement test being prepared. If the test is to be criterion referenced, item difficulty is determined by the difficulty of the learning tasks described in the specific learning outcomes. If the test is to be norm referenced, item difficulty is deliberately altered to obtain a wide spread of test scores. These different approaches to item difficulty constitute one of the major distinctions between criterion referenced and norm referenced testing.

Because a criterion referenced test is designed to describe the specific learning tasks an individual can and cannot perform, item difficulty should match the difficulty of the task. If the task is easy, the test items should be easy. If the task is difficult, the test items should be difficult. No item should be eliminated simply because most students might be expected to answer it correctly or because it might be answered incorrectly by most students. Likewise no attempt should be made to alter item difficulty to obtain a spread of test scores. What we seek in a criterion referenced test is a set of test items that can be used to describe how well a student performs on a clearly defined domain of learning tasks, without reference to the performance of others. To serve this function effectively, the test items must match the learning tasks as closely as possible in all respects, including item difficulty.

Norm referenced achievement tests are designed to rank individuals in order of their achievement. For this purpose a wide spread of test scores is desired so that a dependable (that is, reliable) ranking is obtained. For example, we can say with greater confidence that Mary has achieved more than Tom if the difference in test scores is ten points rather than two. Thus, the ability of test items to discriminate among students is vital to norm-referenced testing, and typically the greater the spread of scores, the better.

The desired score variability in norm-referenced tests is obtained by eliminating the very easy items (those likely to be answered correctly by all students) and by constructing the majority of items at an average level of difficulty, that is, a level at which approximately one half of the students answer correctly. Although some easy items may be desirable at the beginning of the test for motivational purposes and some difficult ones at the end to challenge the high achievers, items of average difficulty should be favored because they provide for maximum discrimination among individuals. This will be described in greater detail in Chapter 7, where item analysis is considered.

In deliberately altering item difficulty in norm-referenced tests to provide for the desired spread of scores, care should be taken to keep the items relevant to the learning outcomes to be measured. In measuring the ability to distinguish between concepts, for example, item difficulty can be increased by calling for finer discriminations. Similarly, in measuring the ability to apply principles to new situations, items can be constructed that call for increasingly complex applications. Item difficulty should not be increased by measuring more obscure material or by overloading the test with items on a particular learning outcome that happens to be difficult. Although a norm-referenced achievement test is designed to rank students from high to low, that ranking should represent the relative degree to which the instructional objectives are being achieved. If irrelevant difficulty is introduced, the items will provide a less valid measure of the intended learning outcomes.

Determining the Number of Items

The test specifications should indicate what sample of items is to be included in the test and thus the number of items to be used. Although the number of items is determined primarily by the purpose of the test and the types of test items to be prepared, there are practical constraints that must also be considered. Two major ones are the age of the students tested and the time available for testing. In the testing of elementary school students, the testing time typically should be no more than 30 minutes so that proper motivation is maintained. At the high school and college levels, students can be given tests lasting several hours (for example, a final examination), but most tests are limited to a testing time of 40 to 50 minutes because of the length of the typical class period.

In matching the number of items to available testing time, we are faced with the problem of estimating how many items students can complete per minute. Unfortunately there are no simple answers. It depends on the type of test item, the complexity of the learning outcome measured, and the age of the students. As a rule of thumb, high school and college students should be able to answer one multiple-choice item, three short-answer items, or three true-false items per minute when the items are measuring knowledge outcomes. For measuring more complex learning outcomes such as comprehension and application, and for testing younger age groups, more time per item is needed. In estimating the number of items to be used, keep in mind the slower students in the group, for it is desirable to give all students an opportunity to complete the test. Experience in testing a given group of students is frequently the only dependable guide for determining proper test length.

In addition to our concern with total test length, consideration must be given to the number of test items needed for each type of interpretation to be made. This issue is especially crucial in criterion-referenced interpretation, where we want to describe student performance in terms of each intended learning outcome. For this purpose we should use at least ten items per outcome. Where practical constraints make it necessary to use fewer than ten items for an intended outcome, only tentative judgments should be made and these should be verified by other means. In some cases it is possible to combine items into larger item clusters for a more meaningful interpretation.

TECHNICAL CONSIDERATIONS IN TEST PLANNING

The two most important characteristics of a well-constructed achievement test are *validity* and *reliability*. These characteristics should be of prime concern during test construction and most of the suggestions in this book are directed toward preparing tests that provide valid and reliable scores.

Validity refers to the degree to which test scores serve their intended use. In the case of achievement testing, we intend to use the scores to describe the extent to which students have achieved the intended learning outcomes. Since we can measure only a sample of the student performance that represents satisfactory achievement of the outcomes, the validity of our scores depends mainly on the adequacy of the test sample. Ideally, our test should provide scores that are based on a representative sample of instructionally relevant tasks. This content-related evidence of validity can best be obtained by following a systematic procedure during test development. This includes (1) clearly defining the domain of learning tasks to be measured, (2) carefully preparing the test specifications, and (3) constructing a representative sample of relevant test items. Unless these procedures are followed, the validity of the test scores will be in doubt.

Reliability refers to the *consistency* of measurement. For example, if a student earns a score of 60 on a test, we would like to be able to say that the 60 accurately represents the student's test performance. Thus, if we tested the student at a different time or with a different sample of equivalent items, we would expect to obtain a similar score. This consistency of measurement would indicate that the score is relatively free from errors of measurement and thus one we can depend on (i.e., it has "rely-ability").

We cannot, of course, expect test performance to be perfectly consistent over different occasions or over different samples of the same achievement domain. Such factors as ambiguities in test items, fluctuations in attention, and luck in guessing can introduce errors that cause test scores to vary. An important goal in testing is to keep these errors of measurement to a minimum so that our test scores are as reliable as possible.

In addition to being important in its own right, reliability is necessary to obtain validity. After all, if an individual's test score fluctuated widely on a given sample of items, we could not expect the test to provide a valid measure of achievement. Thus, *reliability provides the consistency that makes validity possible*. It should be noted, of course, that consistency of results is just one important requirement for validity. We could be consistently measuring the wrong thing or using the scores inappropriately. Thus, reliability is a necessary, but not a sufficient, condition for validity.

Both the validity and the reliability of a test can be "built in" during test construction. When we select a representative sample of learning tasks to include in our test, we are providing for validity. When we include an adequate number of items in our test, we are providing for reliability. When we construct relevant test items that are free from ambiguity, clues, and other technical defects, we are providing for both improved validity and reliability. In fact, most of the suggestions for constructing achievement tests presented in this book are directed toward improving the validity and reliability of our test scores.

A more detailed discussion of validity and reliability and methods for determining them is presented in Chapter 9. Although high quality achievement tests can be constructed without this technical background, a fuller understanding of these basic concepts contributes to improved skill in test construction and test interpretation.

OTHER CONSIDERATIONS IN TEST PLANNING

In this chapter, we have emphasized those aspects of test planning that are concerned with the preparation of an achievement test that measures a balanced sample of clearly defined learning outcomes. A complete test plan will, of course, also consider such things as test directions, arrangement of the items in the test, scoring, and whether to correct for guessing. These and similar factors will be discussed in Chapter 7, after we have described the procedures for writing the various types of items that are typically used in achievement tests.

SUMMARY OF POINTS

The emphasis in this chapter can be summarized by the following points.

1. Test planning should be guided by the nature of the learning tasks to be measured and the use to be made of the results.
2. Test planning should include defining the intended learning outcomes in terms of student performance.
3. Test specifications should be prepared before writing or selecting test items.
4. Test specifications can vary from a two-fold table to a detailed description of the achievement to be measured and the nature of the test to be used.
5. The types of items used in a test should be determined by how directly they measure the intended learning outcomes and how effective they are as measuring instruments.
6. Each test item should provide a task that matches the student performance described in a specific learning outcome.
7. The functioning content of test items can be improved by eliminating irrelevant barriers and unintended clues during item writing.
8. For criterion-referenced interpretation, the difficulty of a test item should match the difficulty of the learning task to be measured.
9. For norm-referenced interpretation, item difficulty may be altered to provide a larger spread of scores, but care must be taken not to introduce irrelevant difficulty (e.g., by using obscure material.)
10. An achievement test should be short enough to permit all students to attempt all items during the testing time available.
11. A test should contain a sufficient number of test items for each type of interpretation to be made. Interpretations based on fewer than ten items should be considered highly tentative.
12. Validity and reliability are the two most important characteristics of achievement testing.
13. An achievement test will provide valid and reliable results if it measures a representative sample of instructionally relevant tasks and provides scores that are relatively free of measurement errors.
14. Validity and reliability are ''built in'' during test construction and, thus, should be considered during all stages of test development.

ADDITIONAL READING

BERK, R. A., ED., *A Guide to Criterion-Referenced Test Construction* (Baltimore, Maryland: Johns Hopkins University Press, 1984). See Chapter 2 by W. J. Popham, "Specifying the Domain of Content or Behaviors" for a description and illustration of criterion-referenced test specifications.

BLOOM, B.S., ED., *et al.*, *Taxonomy of Educational Objectives: Cognitive Domain* (New York: David McKay Co., Inc., 1956). Describes and illustrates the categories in the cognitive domain.

GRONLUND, N.E., *Measurement and Evaluation in Teaching*, 5th ed. (New York: Macmillan Publishing Co., Inc., 1985). See Chapter 2, "Preparing Instructional Objectives" and Chapter 5, "Planning the Classroom Test" for a comprehensive description of how to define intended learning outcomes and their role in planning classroom achievement tests. See the appendix for a description of the cognitive, affective, and psychomotor taxonomies.

GRONLUND, N. E., *Stating Objectives for Classroom Instruction*, 3rd ed. (New York: Macmillan Publishing Co., Inc., 1985). Describes and illustrates how to state instructional objectives as intended learning outcomes. Includes a summary of the cognitive, affective, and psychomotor taxonomies with illustrative objectives and a list of performance terms for each of the categories.

POPHAM, W. J., *Criterion-Referenced Measurement* (Englewood Cliffs, N.J.: Prentice-Hall, Inc., 1978). See Chapter 6, "Preparing Criterion-Referenced Test Specifications" for illustrative specifications for criterion-referenced tests.

ROID, G., AND T. HALADYNA, *A Technology of Test-Item Writing* (New York: Academic Press, 1981). Describes new methods for writing criterion-referenced test items.

3

Constructing Selection Items

Multiple-choice

The multiple-choice item can be used to measure various types of achievement, such as . . . knowledge outcomes . . . comprehension outcomes . . . and
application outcomes. Following simple but important rules for item writing can
improve the quality of the items.

The multiple-choice item is the most widely used and highly regarded of the selection-type items. They can be designed to measure a variety of learning outcomes,
from simple to complex, and can provide the highest quality items. Because they
play such an important role in achievement testing, they will be treated in this
chapter in considerable detail. Other selection-type items (true-false, matching, and
interpretive exercise) will be described in the following chapter.

NATURE OF MULTIPLE-CHOICE ITEMS

The multiple-choice item consists of a *stem*, which presents a problem situation,
and several *alternatives* (*options* or *choices*), which provide possible solutions to
the problem. The stem may be a question or an incomplete statement. The alternatives include the correct answer and several plausible wrong answers called
distracters. The function of the latter is to distract those students who are uncertain
of the answer.

The following items illustrate the question form and the incomplete-statement
form of a multiple-choice item.

EXAMPLE

Which one of the following item types is an example of a supply-type test item?

   A. Multiple-choice item.
   B. True-false item.
   C. Matching item.
*D. Short-answer item.

An example of a supply-type test item is the:

   A. multiple-choice item.
   B. true-false item.
   C. matching item.
*D. short-answer item.

Although stated differently, both stems pose the same problem. Note, however, that the incomplete statement is more concise. This is typically the case. The question form is easier to write and forces the test maker to pose a clear problem but tends to result in a longer stem. An effective procedure for the beginner is to start with a question and shift to the incomplete statement whenever greater conciseness can be obtained.

The alternatives in the above examples contain only one correct answer, and the distracters are clearly incorrect. Another type of multiple-choice item is the *best-answer* form, in which the alternatives are all partially correct but one is clearly better than the others. This type is used for more complex achievement, as when the student must select the best reason for an action, the best method for doing something, or the best application of a principle. Thus, whether the correct-answer or best-answer form is used depends on the learning outcomes to be measured.

EXAMPLE

Which item type is *best* for measuring computational skill?

   A. Multiple-choice item.
   B. True-false item.
   C. Matching item.
*D. Short-answer item.

The examples given illustrate the use of four alternatives. Multiple-choice items typically include either three, four, or five choices. The larger number will, of course, reduce the student's chances of obtaining the correct answer by guessing.

Theoretically, with five alternatives there is only one chance in five of guessing the answer, whereas with four alternatives there is one chance in four. It is frequently difficult to obtain five plausible choices, however, and items are not improved by adding obviously wrong answers merely to have five alternatives. There is no reason why the items in a given test should all have the same number of alternatives. Some might contain three, some four, and some five, depending on the availability of plausible distracters. This would pose a problem only if the test were to be corrected for guessing, a practice, as we see later, that is not recommended for informal achievement tests.

USES OF MULTIPLE-CHOICE ITEMS

The multiple-choice item can be used to measure knowledge outcomes and various types of complex learning outcomes. The single-item format is probably most widely used for measuring knowledge, comprehension, and application outcomes. The interpretive exercise consisting of a series of multiple-choice items based on introductory material (e.g., paragraph, picture, or graph) is especially useful for measuring analysis, interpretation, and other complex learning outcomes. The interpretive exercise will be described in the following chapter. Here, we confine the discussion to the use of single, independent, multiple-choice items.

Knowledge Items

Knowledge items typically measure the degree to which previously learned material has been remembered. The items focus on the simple recall of information and can be concerned with the measurement of terms, facts, or other specific aspects of knowledge.

EXAMPLES

Outcome: Identifies the meaning of a term.
    Reliability means the same as:
        *A   consistency
        B   relevancy
        C   representativeness
        D   usefulness

Outcome: Identifies the order of events.
    What is the first step in constructing an achievement test?
        A.   Decide on test length.
        *B.   Identify the intended learning outcomes.
        C.   Prepare a table of specifications.
        D.   Select the item types to use.

The wide varity of knowledge outcomes that can be measured with multiple-choice items is best shown by illustrating some of the types of questions that can be

*ILLUSTRATIVE KNOWLEDGE QUESTIONS**

1.11. *Knowledge of Terminology*
What word means the same as _____?
Which statement best defines the term _____?
In this sentence, what is the meaning of the word _____?

1.12 *Knowledge of Specific Facts*
Where would you find _____?
Who first discovered _____?
What is the name of _____?

1.21 *Knowledge of Conventions*
What is the correct form for_____?
Which statement indicates correct usage of _____?
Which of the following rules applies to _____?

1.22 *Knowledge of Trends and Sequences*
Which of the following best describes the trend of _____?
What is the most important cause of _____?
Which of the following indicates the proper order of _____?

1.23 *Knowledge of Classifications and Categories*
What are the main types of _____?
What are the major classifications of _____?
What are the characteristics of _____?

1.24 *Knowledge of Criteria*
Which of the following is a criterion for judging _____?
What is the most important criterion for selecting _____?
What criteria are used to classify _____?

1.25 *Knowledge of Methodology*
What method is used for _____?
What is the best way to_____?
What would be the first step in making _____?

1.31 *Knowledge of Principles and Generalizations*
Which statement best expresses the principle of _____?
Which statement best summarizes the belief that _____?
Which of the following principles best explains _____?

1.32 *Knowledge of Theories and Structures*
Which statement is most consistent with the theory of _____?
Which of the following best describes the structure of _____?
What evidence best supports the theory of _____?

*Based on *Taxonomy of Educational Objectives* (see Chapter 2).

---

asked in various knowledge categories. Sample questions stated as incomplete multiple-choice stems are presented in the accompanying box.

The series of questions shown in the box, of course, provides only a sample of the many possible questions that could be asked. Also the questions are stated in rather general terms. The stems for multiple-choice items need to be more closely related to the specific learning outcome being measured.

Comprehension Items

Comprehension items typically measure at the lowest level of understanding. They determine whether the students have grasped the meaning of the material without requiring them to apply it. Comprehension can be measured by requiring students to respond in various ways but it is important that the items contain some *novelty*. The following test items illustrate the measurement of common types of learning outcomes at the comprehension level.

EXAMPLE

Outcome: Identifies an example of a term.
  Which one of the following statements contains a *specific determiner?*
      A.   America is a continent.
      B.   America was discovered in 1492.
    *C.   America has some big industries.
      D.   America's population is increasing.

EXAMPLE

Outcome: Interprets the meaning of an idea.
  The statement that "test reliability is a necessary but not a sufficient condition of test validity" means that:
      A.   a reliable test will have a certain degree of validity.
    *B.   a valid test will have a certain degree of reliability.
      C.   a reliable test may be completely invalid and a valid test completely unreliable.

EXAMPLE

Outcome: Identifies an example of a concept or principle.
  Which of the following is an example of a criterion-referenced interpretation?
      A.   Derik earned the highest score in science.
      B.   Erik completed his experiment faster than his classmates.
      C.   Edna's test score was higher than 50 percent of the class.
    *D.   Tricia set up her laboratory equipment in five minutes.

EXAMPLE

Outcome: Predicts the most probable effect of an action.
  What is most likely to happen to the reliability of the scores for a multiple-choice test, where the number of alternatives for each item is changed from three to four?
      A.   It will decrease.
    *B.   It will increase.
      C.   It will stay the same.
      D.   There is no basis for making a prediction.

In this last example, the student must recognize that increasing the number of alternatives in the items produces the same effect as lengthening the test.

These examples would, of course, represent measurement at the comprehension level only where the situations were new to the students. If the solutions to these particular problems were encountered during instruction, the items would need to be classified as knowledge outcomes.

Some of the many learning outcomes at the comprehension level that can be measured by multiple-choice items are illustrated by the incomplete questions in the accompanying box.

ILLUSTRATIVE COMPREHENSION AND APPLICATION QUESTIONS

Comprehension Questions

Which of the following is an example of _____ ?

What is the main thought expressed by _____ ?

What are the main differences between _____ ?

What are the common characteristics of _____ ?

Which of the following is another form of _____ ?

Which of the following best explains _____ ?

Which of the following best summarizes _____ ?

Which of the following best illustrates _____ ?

What do you predict would happen if _____ ?

What trend do you predict in _____ ?

Application Questions

Which of the following methods is best for _____ ?

What steps should be followed in applying _____ ?

Which situation would require the use of _____ ?

Which principle would be best for solving _____ ?

What procedure is best for improving _____ ?

What procedure is best for constructing _____ ?

What procedure is best for correcting _____ ?

Which of the following is the best plan for _____ ?

Which of the following provides the proper sequence for _____ ?

What is the most probable effect of _____ ?

Application Items

Application items also measure understanding, but typically at a higher level than that of comprehension. Here, the students must demonstrate that they not only grasp the meaning of information, but can also apply it to concrete situations that are new to them. Thus, application items determine the extent to which students can transfer their learning and use it effectively in solving new problems. Such items may call for the application of various aspects of knowledge, such as facts, concepts, principles, rules, methods, and theories. Both comprehension and application items are adaptable to practically all areas of subject matter, and they provide the basic means of measuring understanding.

The following examples illustrate the use of multiple-choice items for measuring learning outcomes at the application level.

EXAMPLE

Outcome: Distinguishes between properly and improperly stated outcomes.
  Which of the following learning outcomes is properly stated in terms of student performance?
    A.   Develops an appreciation of the importance of testing.
    *B.   Explains the purpose of test specifications.
    C.   Learns how to write good test items.
    D.   Realizes the importance of validity.

EXAMPLE

Outcome: Improves defective test items.
  Directions: Read the following test item and then indicate the best change to make to improve the item.
                Which one of the following types of learning outcomes is most difficult to evaluate objectively?
                    1.   A concept.
                    2.   An application.
                    3.   An appreciation.
                    4.   None of the above

The best change to make in the previous item would be to:
    A.   change the stem to incomplete-statement form.
    B.   use letters instead of numbers for each alternative.
    C.   remove the indefinite articles "a" and "an" from the alternatives.
    *D.   replace "none of the above" with "an interpretation."

When writing application items, care must be taken to select problems that the students have not encountered previously and therefore cannot solve on the basis of general knowledge alone. Each item should be so designed that it calls for application of the particular fact, concept, principle, or procedure indicated in the intended learning outcome. See the accompanying box for some of the many questions that might be asked at the application level.

RULES FOR WRITING MULTIPLE-CHOICE ITEMS

An effective multiple-choice item presents students with a task that is both important and clearly understood, and one that can be answered correctly by anyone who has achieved the intended learning outcome. Nothing in the content or structure of the item should prevent an informed student from responding correctly. Similarly, nothing in the content or structure of the item should enable an uninformed student to select the correct answer. The following rules for item writing are intended as guides for the preparation of multiple-choice items that function as intended.

1. Design each item to measure an important learning outcome. The problem situation around which an item is to be built should be important and should be related to the intended learning outcome to be measured. The items in the previous section illustrate how to match items to intended outcomes. When writing the item, focus on the functioning content of the item and resist the temptation to include irrelevant material or more obscure and less significant content to increase item difficulty. Remember that the purpose of each item is to call forth the type of performance that will help determine the extent to which the intended learning outcomes have been achieved.

Items designed to measure complex achievement must contain some novelty. For example, where a knowledge item might require the identification of a textbook definition of a term, a comprehension item may require the identification of a modified form of it, and an application item may require the identification of an example of its proper use. Both the comprehension and application items would function as intended, however, only if the material was new to the students. Thus, items measuring complex achievement should require students to demonstrate that they have grasped the meaning of the material and can use it in situations that are new to them.

2. Present a single clearly formulated problem in the stem of the item. The task set forth in the stem of the item should be so clear that a student can understand it without reading the alternatives. In fact, a good check on the clarity and completeness of a multiple-choice stem is to cover the alternatives and determine whether it could be answered without the choices. Try this on the two sample items that follow.

EXAMPLE

Poor: A table of specifications:
        A. indicates how a test will be used to improve learning.
     *B. provides a more balanced sampling of content.
        C. arranges the instructional objectives in order of their importance.
        D. specifies the method of scoring to be used on a test.

Better: What is the main advantage of using a table of specifications when preparing an achievement test?
        A. It reduces the amount of time required.
     *B. It improves the sampling of content.
        C. It makes the construction of test items easier.
        D. It increases the objectivity of the test.

The first of these examples is no more than a collection of true-false statements with a common stem. The problem presented in the stem of the improved version is clear enough to serve as a supply-type short-answer item. The alternatives simply provide a series of possible answers from which to choose.

Note also in the second version that a *single* problem is presented in the stem. Including more than one problem usually adds to the complexity of the wording and reduces the diagnostic value of the item. When students *fail* such an item, there is no way to determine which of the problems prevented them from responding correctly.

3. State the stem of the item in simple, clear language.   The problem in the stem of a multiple-choice item should be stated as precisely as possible and should be free of unnecessarily complex wording and sentence structure. Anyone who possesses the knowledge measured by a test item should be able to select the correct answer. Poorly stated item stems frequently introduce sufficient ambiguity to prevent a knowledgeable student from responding correctly. Also, complex sentence structure may make the item a measure more of reading comprehension than of the intended outcome. The first of the two examples that follow is an extreme instance of this problem.

EXAMPLE

Poor: The paucity of plausible, but incorrect, statements that can be related to a central idea poses a problem when constructing which one of the following types of test items?
    A. Short-answer.
    B. True-false.
   *C. Multiple-choice.
    D. Essay.

Better: The lack of plausible, but incorrect, alternatives will cause the greatest difficulty when constructing:
    A. short-answer items.
    B. true-false items.
   *C. multiple-choice items.
    D. essay items.

Another common fault in stating multiple-choice items is to load the stem with irrelevant and, thus, nonfunctioning material. This is probably caused by the instructor's desire to continue to teach the students—even while testing them. The following example illustrates the use of an item stem as "another chance to inform students."

EXAMPLE

Poor: Testing can contribute to the instructional program of the school in many important ways. However, the main function of testing in teaching is:

Better: The main function of testing in teaching is:

The first version increases reading time and makes no contribution to the measurement of the specific outcome. Time spent in reading such irrelevant material could be spent more profitably in thinking about the problem presented. But if the purpose of an item is to measure a student's ability to distinguish between relevant and irrelevant material, this rule must, of course, be disregarded.

4. Put as much of the wording as possible in the stem of the item. Avoid repeating the same material in each of the alternatives. By moving all of the common content to the stem, it is usually possible to clarify the problem further and to reduce the time the student needs to read the alternatives. Note the improvement in the following item when this rule is followed.

EXAMPLE

Poor: In *objective* testing, the term *objective:*
      A. refers to the method of identifying the learning outcomes.
      B. refers to the method of selecting the test content.
      C. refers to the method of presenting the problem.
   *D. refers to the method of scoring the answers.

Better: In *objective* testing, the term *objective* refers to the method of:
      A. identifying the learning outcomes.
      B. selecting the test content.
      C. presenting the problem.
   *D. scoring the answers.

In many cases the problem is not simply to move the common words to the stem, but to reword the entire item. The following examples illustrate how an item can be improved by revising the stem and shortening the alternatives.

EXAMPLE

Poor: Instructional objectives are most apt to be useful for test-construction purposes when they are stated in such a way that they show:
      A. the course content to be covered during the instructional period.
   *B. the kinds of performance students should demonstrate upon reaching the goal.
      C. the things the teacher will do to obtain maximum student learning.
      D. the types of learning activities to be participated in during the course.

Better: Instructional objectives are most useful for test-construction purposes when they are stated in terms of:
      A. course content.
   *B. student performance.
      C. teacher behavior.
      D. learning activities.

It is, of course, impossible to streamline all items in this manner, but economy of wording and clarity of expression are important goals to strive for in test construction.

5. State the stem of the item in positive form, wherever possible. A positively phrased test item tends to measure more important learning outcomes than a negatively stated item. This is because knowing such things as the *best* method or the *most relevant* argument typically has greater educational significance than knowing the *poorest* method or the *least relevant* argument. The use of negatively stated item stems results all too frequently from the ease with which such items can be constructed rather than from the importance of the learning outcomes measured. The test maker who becomes frustrated by the inability to think of a sufficient number of plausible distracters for an item, as in the first following example, suddenly realizes how simple it would be to construct the second version.

EXAMPLE

Item one: Which one of the following is a category in the taxonomy of the cognitive domain?
   *A.   Comprehension.
   B.   *(distracter needed)*
   C.   *(distracter needed)*
   D.   *(distracter needed)*

Item two: Which one of the following is *not* a category in the taxonomy of the cognitive domain?
   A.   Comprehension.
   B.   Application.
   C.   Analysis.
   *D.   *(answer needed)*

Note in the second version that the categories of the taxonomy serve as distracters and that all that is needed to complete the item is a correct answer. This could be any term that appears plausible but is *not* one of the categories listed in the taxonomy. Although such items are easily constructed, they are apt to have a low level of difficulty and are likely to measure relatively unimportant learning outcomes. Being able to identify answers that do *not* apply provides no assurance that the student possesses the desired knowledge.

This solution to the lack of sufficient distracters is most likely to occur when the test maker is committed to the use of multiple-choice items only. A more desirable procedure for measuring the "ability to recognize the categories in the taxonomy of the cognitive domain" is to switch to a modified true-false form, as in the following example.

EXAMPLE

Directions: Indicate which of the following are categories in the taxonomy of the cognitive domain, by circling Y for *yes* and N for *no*.
   *Y N   Comprehension.
   Y N*   Critical thinking.
   Y N*   Reasoning.
   *Y N   Synthesis.

In responding to this item, the student must make a separate judgment for each statement—the statement either is, or is not, one of the categories. Thus, the item calls for the type of performance stated in the learning outcome, yet it avoids the problems of an insufficient number of distracters and of negative phrasing.

6. Emphasize negative wording whenever it is used in the stem of an item. In some instances the use of negative working is basic to the measurement of an important learning outcome. Knowing that you should *not* cross the street against a red light or should *not* mix certain chemicals, for example, is so important that these precepts might be directly taught and directly tested. Any potentially dangerous situation may require a negative emphasis. There are also, of course, less dire circumstances where negative phrasing is useful. Almost any set of rules or procedures places some emphasis on practices to be avoided.

When negative wording is used in the stem of an item, it should be emphasized by being underlined or capitalized and by being placed near the end of the statement:

EXAMPLE

Poor: Which one of the following is not a desirable practice when preparing multiple-choice items?
  A. Stating the stem in positive form.
  B. Using a stem that could function as a short-answer item.
  C. Underlining certain words in the stem for emphasis.
  *D. Shortening the stem by lengthening the alternatives.

Better: All of the following are desirable practices when preparing multiple-choice items EXCEPT:
  A. stating the stem in positive form.
  B. using a stem that could function as a short-answer item.
  C. underlining certain words in the stem for emphasis.
  *D. shortening the stem by lengthening the alternatives.

The improved version of this item assures that the item's negative aspect will not be overlooked, and it furnishes the student with the proper mind-set just before reading the alternatives.

7. Make certain that the intended answer is correct or clearly best.   When the correct-answer form of multiple-choice item is used, there should be only one correct answer and it should be unquestionably correct. With the best-answer form, the intended answer should be one that competent authorities would agree is clearly the best. In the latter case it may also be necessary to include ''of the following'' in the stem of the item to allow for equally satisfactory answers that have not been included in the item:

EXAMPLE

Poor: What is the best method of selecting course content for test items?
Better: Which one of the following is the best method of selecting course content for test items?

The proper phrasing of the stem of an item can also help avoid equivocal answers when the correct-answer form is used. In fact, an inadequately stated problem frequently makes the intended answer only partially correct or makes more than one alternative suitable.

EXAMPLE

Poor: What is the purpose of classroom testing?
Better: One purpose of classroom testing is:
                        (or)
            The main purpose of classroom testing is:

It is, of course, also necessary to check each of the distracters in the item to make certain that none of them could be defended as the correct answer. This will not only improve the quality of the item, but will also prevent a disruptive argument during the discussion of the test results.

8. Make all alternatives grammatically consistent with the stem of the item and parallel in form.   The correct answer is usually carefully phrased so that it is grammatically consistent with the stem. Where the test maker is apt to slip is in stating the distracters. Unless care is taken to check them against the wording in the stem and in the correct answer, they may be inconsistent in tense, article, or grammatical form. This, of course, could provide a clue to the correct answer, or at least make some of the distracters ineffective.

A general step that can be taken to prevent grammatical inconsistency is to avoid using the articles ''a'' or ''an'' at the end of the stem of the item:

EXAMPLE

Poor: The recall of factual information can be measured best with a:
       A.   matching item.
       B.   multiple-choice item.
    *C.   short-answer item.
       D.   essay question.

Better: The recall of factual information can be measured best with:
       A.   matching items.
       B.   multiple-choice items.
    *C.   short-answer items .
       D.   essay questions.

The indefinite article ''a'' in the first version makes the last distracter obviously wrong. By simply changing the alternatives from singular to plural, it is possible to omit the article. In other cases, it may be necessary to add an article (''a,'' ''an,'' or as appropriate) to each alternative or to rephrase the entire item.

Stating all of the alternatives in parallel form also tends to prevent unnecessary clues from being given to the students. When the grammatical structure of one alternative differs from that of the others, some students may more readily detect that alternative as a correct or an incorrect response:

EXAMPLE

Poor: Why should negative terms be avoided in the stem of a multiple-choice item?
     *A.   They may be overlooked.
     B.   The stem tends to be longer.
     C.   The construction of alternatives is more difficult.
     D.   The scoring is more difficult.

Better: Why should negative terms be avoided in the stem of a multiple-choice item?
     *A.   They may be overlooked.
     B.   They tend to increase the length of the stem.
     C.   They make the construction of alternatives more difficult.
     D.   They may increase the difficulty of the scoring.

In the first version some students who lack the knowledge called for are apt to select the correct answer because of the way it is stated. The parallel grammatical structure in the second version removes this clue.

9. Avoid verbal clues that might enable students to select the correct answer or to eliminate an incorrect alternative.   One of the most common sources of extraneous clues in multiple-choice items is the wording of the item. Some such clues are rather obvious and are easily avoided. Others require the constant attention of the test maker to prevent them from slipping in unnoticed. Let's review some of the verbal clues commonly found in multiple-choice items.

(a) *Similarity of wording in both the stem and the correct answer* is one of the most obvious clues. Key words in the stem may unintentionally be repeated verbatim in the correct answer, a synonym may be used, or the words may simply sound or look alike:

EXAMPLE

Poor: Which one of the following would you consult first to locate research articles on achievement testing?
     A.   *Journal of Educational Psychology*
     B.   *Journal of Educational Measurement*
     C.   *Journal of Consulting Psychology*
     *D.   *Review of Educational Research*

The word "research" in both the stem and the correct answer is apt to provide a clue to the correct answer to the uninformed but testwise student. Such obvious clues might better be used in both the stem and an *incorrect* answer, in order to lead the uninformed *away* from the correct answer.

(b) *Stating the correct answer in textbook language or stereotyped phraseology* may cause students to select it because it looks better than the other alternatives, or because they vaguely recall having seen it before:

EXAMPLE

Poor: Learning outcomes are most useful in preparing tests when they are:
   *A.   clearly stated in performance terms.
   B.   developed cooperatively by teachers and students.
   C.   prepared after the instruction has ended.
   D.   stated in general terms.

The pat phrasing of the correct answers is likely to give it away. Even the most poorly prepared student is apt to recognize the often repeated phrase "clearly stated in performance terms," without having the foggiest notion of what it means.

(c) *Stating the correct answer in greater detail* may provide a clue. Also, when the answer is qualified by modifiers that are typically associated with true statements (for example, "sometimes," "may," "usually"), it is more likely to be chosen:

EXAMPLE

Poor: Lack of attention to learning outcomes during test preparation:
   A.   will lower the technical quality of the items.
   B.   will make the construction of test items more difficult.
   C.   will result in the greater use of essay questions.
   *D.   may result in a test that is less relevant to the instructional program.

The term "may" is rather obvious in this example, but this type of error is common and appears frequently in a subtler form.

(d) *Including absolute terms in the distracters* enables students to eliminate them as possible answers because such terms ("always," "never," "all," "none," "only,") are commonly associated with false statements. This makes the correct answer obvious, or at least increases the chances that the students who do not know the answer will guess it:

EXAMPLE

Poor: Achievement tests help students improve their learning by:
   A.   encouraging them all to study hard.
   *B.   informing them of their progress.
   C.   giving them all a feeling of success.
   D.   preventing any of them from neglecting their assignments.

Such absolutes tend to be used by the inexperienced test maker to assure that the incorrect alternatives are clearly wrong. Unfortunately they are easily recognized by the student as unlikely answers, making them ineffective as distracters.

(e) *Including two responses that are all inclusive* makes it possible to eliminate the other alternatives, since one of the two must obviously be the correct answer:

EXAMPLE

Poor: Which one of the following types of test items measures learning outcomes at the recall level?
  - *A.   Supply-type items.
  - B.   Selection-type items.
  - C.   Matching items.
  - D.   Multiple-choice items.

Since the first two alternatives include the only two major types of test items, even poorly prepared students are likely to limit their choices to these two. This, of course, gives them a fifty-fifty chance of guessing the correct answer.

(f) *Including two responses that have the same meaning* makes it possible to eliminate them as potential answers. If two alternatives have the same meaning and only one answer is to be selected, it is fairly obvious that both alternatives must be incorrect:

EXAMPLE

Poor: Which one of the following is the most important characteristic of achievement-test results?
  - A.   Consistency.
  - B.   Reliability.
  - *C.   Relevance.
  - D.   Objectivity.

In this item both "consistency" and "reliability" can be eliminated because they mean essentially the same thing.

Extraneous clues to the correct answer must be excluded from test items if the items are to function as intended. It is frequently good practice, however, to use such clues to lead the uninformed away from the correct answer. If not overdone, this can contribute to the plausibility of the incorrect alternatives.

10. Make the distracters plausible and attractive to the uninformed.   The distracters in a multiple- choice item should be so appealing to the students who lack the knowledge called for by the item that they select one of the distracters in preference to the correct answer. This is the ideal, of course, but one toward which the test maker must work continually. The art of constructing good multiple-choice items depends heavily on the development of effective distracters.

You can do a number of things to increase the plausibility and attractiveness of distracters:

a. Use the common misconceptions or errors of students as distracters.
b. State the alternatives in the language of the student.
c. Use "good-sounding" words ("accurate," "important,") in the distracters as well as in the correct answer.
d. Make the distracters similar to the correct answer in both length and complexity of wording.
e. Use extraneous clues in the distracters, such as stereotyped phrasing, scientific sounding answers, and verbal associations with the stem of the item. But don't overuse these clues to the point where they become ineffective.
f. Make the alternatives homogeneous, but in doing so beware of fine discriminations that are educationally insignificant.

The greater plausibility resulting from the use of more homogenous alternatives can be seen in the improved version of the following item.

EXAMPLE

Poor: Obtaining a dependable ranking of students is of major concern when using:
   *A. norm-referenced summative tests.
   B. behavior descriptions.
   C. check lists.
   D. questionnaires.

Better: Obtaining a dependable ranking of students is of major concern when using:
   *A. norm-referenced summative tests.
   B. teacher-made diagnostic tests.
   C. mastery achievement tests.
   D. criterion-referenced formative tests.

The improved version not only increases the plausibility of the distracters; it also calls for a type of discrimination that is more educationally significant.

11. Vary the relative length of the correct answer to eliminate length as a clue.   There is a tendency for the correct answer to be longer than the alternatives because of the need to qualify statements to make them unequivocally correct. This, of course, provides a clue to the testwise student. Learning this fact, the inexperienced test maker frequently makes a special effort to avoid ever having the correct answer longer than the other alternatives. This, of course, also provides a clue, and the alert student soon learns to dismiss the longest alternative as a possible answer.

The relative length of the correct answer can be removed as a clue by varying it in such a manner that no apparent pattern is provided. That is, it should sometimes be longer, sometimes shorter, and sometimes of equal length—but never consistently or predominantly of one relative length. In some cases it is more desirable to make the alternatives approximately equal length by adjusting the distracters rather than the correct answer:

EXAMPLE

Poor: One advantage of multiple-choice items over essay questions is that they:
    A. measure more complex outcomes.
    B. depend more on recall.
    C. require less time to score.
  *D. provide for a more extensive sampling of course content.

Better: One advantage of multiple-choice items over essay questions is that they:
    A. provide for the measurement of more complex learning outcomes.
    B. place greater emphasis on the recall of factual information.
    C. require less time for test preparation and scoring.
  *D. provide for a more extensive sampling of course content.

Lengthening the distracters, as was done in the improved version, both removes length as a clue and increases the plausibility of the distracters, which are now more similar to the correct answer in complexity of wording.

12. Avoid using the alternative "all of the above," and use "none of the above" with extreme caution.   When test makers are having difficulty in locating a sufficient number of distracters, they frequently resort to the use of "all of the above" or "none of the above" as the final option. These special alternatives are seldom used appropriately and almost always render the item less effective than it would be without them.

The inclusion of "all of the above" as an option makes it possible to answer the item on the basis of partial information. Since students are to select only one answer, they can detect "all of the above" as the correct choice simply by noting that two of the alternatives are correct. They can also detect it as a wrong answer by recognizing that at least one of the alternatives is incorrect; of course, their chance of guessing the correct answer from the remaining choices then increases proportionately. Another difficulty with this option is that some students, recognizing that the first choice is correct, will select it without reading the remaining alternatives.

Obviously the use of "none of the above" is not possible with the best-answer type of multiple-choice item, since the alternatives vary in appropriateness and the criterion of absolute correctness is not applicable. When used as the right answer in a correct-answer type of item, this option may be measuring nothing more than the ability to detect incorrect answers. Recognizing that certain answers are wrong is no guarantee that the student knows what is correct. For example, a student may be able to answer the following item correctly without being able to name the categories in the taxonomy:

> *Poor:*   Which of the following is a category in the taxonomy of the cognitive domain?
>   A.   Critical thinking.
>   B.   Scientific thinking.
>   C.   Reasoning ability.
>   *D.   None of above.

All students need to know to answer this item correctly is that the taxonomy categories are new and different from those that they have commonly associated with intellectual skills. Items such as this provide rather poor evidence for judging a student's achievement.

The alternative "none of the above" is probably used most widely with computational problems that are presented in multiple-choice form. The publishers of standardized achievement tests have resorted to multiple-choice items for such problems in order to make machine scoring possible, and they have resorted to the alternative "none of the above" in order to reduce the likelihood of the student estimating the answer without performing the entire computation. Although this use of "none of the above" may be defensible, there is seldom a need to use multiple-choice items for computational problems in classroom tests. The supply-type item which requires the student to solve the problems and record the answers provides the most direct and useful measure of computational skill. This is another case in which it is desirable to switch from multiple-choice items to another item type in order to obtain more effective measurement.

13. Vary the position of the correct answer in a random manner.   The correct answer should appear in each alternative position about the same number of times, but its placement should not follow a pattern that may be apparent to the person taking the test. Students who detect that the correct answer never appears in the same position more than twice in a row, or that A is the correct answer on every fourth item, are likely to obtain a higher score than their knowledge would warrant. Such clues can be avoided by random placement of the correct answer.

The easiest way to randomly assign the position of the correct answer in a multiple-choice item is to develop a code with the aid of a book: simply open any book at a random place, look at the right-hand page, and let the last digit of the page number determine the placement of the correct answer. Since the right-hand page always ends in an odd number, the code might be as follows: the digit 1 indicates that the correct answer will be placed in position A, 3 = B, 5 = C, 7 = D, and 9 = E.

Sufficient variation without a discernible pattern might also be obtained by simply placing the responses in alphabetical order, based on the first letter in each, and letting the correct answer fall where it will.

When the alternative responses are numbers, they should always be listed in order of size, preferably in ascending order. This will eliminate the possibility of a clue, such as the correct answer being the only one that is not in numerical order.

14. Control the difficulty of the item either by varying the problem in the stem or by changing the alternatives. It is usually preferable to increase item difficulty by increasing the level of knowledge called for by making the problem more complex. However, it is also possible to increase difficulty by making the alternatives more homogeneous. When this is done, care must be taken that the finer discriminations called for are educationally significant and are in harmony with the learning outcomes to be measured.

15. Make certain each item is independent of the other items in the test. Occasionally information given in the stem of one item will help the students answer another item. This can be remedied easily by a careful review of the items before they are assembled into a test.

A different type of problem occurs when the correct answer to an item depends upon knowing the correct answer to the item preceding it. The student who is unable to answer the first item, of course, has no basis for responding to the second. Such chains of interlocking items should be avoided. Each item should be an independently scorable unit.

16. Use an efficient item format. The alternatives should be listed on separate lines, under one another, like the examples in this chapter. This makes the alternatives easy to read and compare. It also contributes to ease of scoring since the letters of the alternatives all appear on the left side of the paper. A copy of the test can be used as a scoring stencil: simply circle the letters of the correct answers on the copy; then place the copy next to the student's paper so that the columns of letters correspond.

The use of letters in front of the alternatives is preferable to the use of numbers, since numerical answers in numbered items may be confusing to the students.

When writing the item, follow the normal rules of grammar. If the stem of the item is a question, each alternative should begin with a capital letter and end with a period or other terminal punctuation mark. The period should be omitted with numerical answers, however, so that they will not be confused with decimal points. When the stem is an incomplete statement, each alternative should begin with a lower-case letter and end with whatever terminal punctuation mark is appropriate.[1]

The sixteen rules given for constructing multiple-choice items are stated rather dogmatically as an aid to the beginner. As experience in test construction is obtained, it will soon be noted that there are exceptions to some of the rules and that minor modifications of other rules may be desirable. Until the gaining of such

---

[1]See checklist in the Appendix for reviewing multiple-choice items.

experience, however, the novice will find that following these rules closely will yield test items of fairly high quality.

SUMMARY OF POINTS

The emphasis in this chapter can be summarized by the following points.

1. The multiple-choice item is the most highly regarded and widely used selection-type item.
2. The multiple-choice item can be designed to measure various types of achievement ranging from simple knowledge outcomes to various types of complex learning.
3. Knowledge items typically measure the simple remembering of material.
4. Comprehension items measure the extent to which students have grasped the meaning of the material.
5. Application items measure whether students can use information in concrete situations.
6. Items designed to measure achievement beyond the knowledge level must contain some novelty.
7. The stem of a multiple-choice item should present a single clearly formulated problem that is related to an important learning outcome.
8. The intended answer should be correct or clearly best, as agreed upon by authorities.
9. The distracters (incorrect alternatives) should be plausible enough to lead the uninformed away from the correct answer.
10. The items should be written in simple, clear language that is free of nonfunctioning content.
11. The items should be free of irrelevant sources of difficulty (e.g., ambiguity) that might prevent an informed examinee from answering correctly.
12. The items should be free of irrelevant clues (e.g., verbal associations) that might enable an uninformed examinee to answer correctly.

ADDITIONAL READING

BLOOM, B. S., MADAUS, G. F. AND J. T. HASTINGS, *Evaluation to Improve Learning* (New York: McGraw-Hill, 1981). See Chapter 8, "Evaluation Techniques for Knowledge and Comprehension Objectives," and Chapter 9, "Evaluation Techniques for Application and Analysis Objectives," for numerous examples of multiple-choice items designed to measure various learning outcomes.

GRONLUND, N. E., *"Measurement and Evaluation in Teaching,"* 5th ed. (New York: Macmillan Publishing Co., Inc., 1985). See Chapter 7, "Constructing Objective Test Items: Multiple-Choice Form," for illustrative test items representing various content areas, learning outcomes, and grade levels.

MEHRENS, W. A. AND I. J. LEHMANN, *Measurement and Evaluation in Education and Psychology,* 3rd ed. (New York: Holt, Rinehart and Winston, Inc., 1984). See Chapter 7, "Writing Objective Test Items: The Multiple-Choice and Context-Dependent Items," for item writing rules and illustrative items.

4

Constructing Selection Items

True-false, matching,

and interpretive exercise

True-false items . . . matching items . . . and interpretive exercises are also useful in achievement testing. . . . Here we shall describe and illustrate the rules for writing these item types.

The multiple-choice item provides the most generally useful format for measuring achievement at various levels of learning. Thus, when selection-type items are to be used, an effective procedure is to start each item as a multiple-choice item and switch to another item type only when the learning outcome and content make it desirable to do so. For example, (1) when there are only two possible alternatives, a shift can be made to a true-false item; (2) when there are a number of similar factors to be related, a shift can be made to a matching item; and (3) when the items are to measure analysis, interpretation, and other complex outcomes, a shift can be made to the interpretive exercise. This procedure makes it possible to use the special strengths of the multiple-choice item and to use the other selection-type items more appropriately.

TRUE-FALSE ITEMS

True-false items are typically used to measure the ability to identify whether statements of fact are correct. The basic format is simply a declarative statement that the student must judge as true or false. There are modifications of this basic form in which the student must respond "yes" or "no," "agree" or "disagree," "right" or "wrong," "fact" or "opinion," and the like. Such variations are usually given the more general name of *alternative-response* items. In any event, this item type is characterized by the fact that only two responses are possible.

EXAMPLE

T *F   True-false items are classified as a supply-type item.

In some cases the student is asked to judge each statement as true or false, and then to change the false statements so that they are true. When this is done, a portion of each statement is underlined to indicate the part that can be changed. In the example given, for instance, the words "supply-type" would be underlined. The key parts of true statements, of course, must also be underlined.

Another variation is the cluster-type true-false format. In this case, a series of items is based on a common stem.

EXAMPLE

Which of the following terms indicates observable student performance? Circle Y for yes and N for no.

  *Y   N 1. Explains
  *Y   N 2. Identifies
   Y *N 3. Learns
  *Y   N 4. Predicts
   Y *N 5. Realizes

This item format is especially useful for replacing multiple-choice items that have more than one correct answer. Such items are impossible to score satisfactorily. This is avoided with the cluster-type item because it makes each alternative a separate scoring unit of one point. In our example, the student must record whether each term does or does not indicate observable student performance. Thus, this set of items provides an even better measure of the "ability to distinguish between performance and nonperformance terms" than would the single answer multiple-choice item. This is a good illustration of the procedure discussed earlier, that is, starting with multiple-choice items and switching to other item types when more effective measurement will result.

The true-false item has a number of characteristics that limits its usefulness in measuring achievement. (1) It is difficult to obtain statements that are unquestionably true or clearly false without the use of qualifiers that provide clues to the answer. (2) Since there are only two possible choices, the uninformed student has a fifty-fifty chance of guessing the answer. This lowers the reliability of the scores. (3) When a student marks a true statement false, there is no way of determining what misconception led to the wrong answer. (4) When a student marks a false statement false, there is no assurance that the student knows the true version (unless required to change the false statement to true). (5) Single item true-false statements are limited largely to measuring knowledge outcomes, although there are a few notable exceptions (e.g., distinguishing between fact and opinion, and identifying cause–effect relations). Many of these problems are avoided with multiple-choice items, where the student must always select the correct or best answer and the chances of guessing it are considerably reduced. In addition, the selection of incorrect alternatives on multiple-choice items provides clues to the types of misconceptions held by students.

Despite the limitations of the true-false item, there are situations where it should be used. Whenever there are only two possible responses, the true-false item, or some adaptation of it, is likely to provide the most effective measure. Situations of this type include a simple "yes" or "no" response in classifying objects, determining whether a rule does or does not apply, distinguishing fact from opinion, and indicating whether arguments are relevant or irrelevant. As we indicated earlier, the best procedure is to use the true-false, or alternative-response, item only when this item type is more appropriate than the multiple-choice form.

Rules for Writing True-False Items

The purpose of a true-false item, as with all item types, is to distinguish between those who have and those who have not achieved the intended learning outcome. Achievers should be able to select the correct alternative without difficulty, while nonachievers should find the incorrect alternative at least as attractive as the correct one. The rules for writing true-false items are directed toward this end.

1. Include only one central idea in each statement. The main point of the item should be in a prominent position in the statement. The true-false decision should not depend on some subordinate point or trivial detail. The use of several ideas in each statement should generally be avoided because these tend to be confusing and the answer is more apt to be influenced by reading ability than the intended outcome.

EXAMPLE

Poor:	T	*F	The true-false item, which is favored by test experts, is also called an alternative-response item.
Better:	*T	F	The true-false item is also called an alternative-response item.

The "poor" example must be marked false because test experts do not favor the true-false item. Such subordinate points are easily overlooked when reading the item. If the point is important, it should be included as the main idea in a separate item.

2. Keep the statement short and use simple vocabulary and sentence structure. A short, simple statement will increase the likelihood that the point of the item is clear. All students should be able to grasp what the statement is saying. Passing or failing the item should depend solely on whether a student has achieved the necessary knowledge.

EXAMPLE

Poor:	*T F	The true-false item is more subject to guessing but it should be used in place of a multiple-choice item, if well constructed, when there is a dearth of distracters that are plausible.
Better:	*T F	The true-false item should be used in place of a multiple-choice item when only two alternatives are possible.

Long, involved statements like the "poor" version tend to contaminate the achievement measure with a measure of reading comprehension. A basic rule of item writing is to focus on the intended function of the item and remove all irrelevant influences.

3. Word the statement so precisely that it can unequivocally be judged true or false.   True statements should be true under all circumstances and yet free of qualifiers ("may," "possible," and so on), which might provide clues. This requires the use of precise words and the avoidance of such vague terms as "seldom," "frequently," and "often." The same care, of course, must also be given to false statements so that their falsity is not too readily apparent from differences in wording.

At first glance, this seems like a simple rule to follow but it causes frequent problems.

EXAMPLE

Poor:	T *F	Lengthening a test will increase its reliability.
Better:	*T F	Lengthening a test by adding items like those in the test will increase its reliability.

The "poor" version of this item must be marked false because it is not true under all conditions. For example, if items are added to the test that all students fail, reliability would not be changed. However, the "poor" version would not be a good item to use in a test because it requires students to mark a very important principle of measurement false. We could say "usually will increase" but the qualifier would encourage those who are uninformed to mark it true and they would receive an unearned point. The "better" version has no such "giveaway" to the answer. In fact, an uninformed student might think that adding similar items to a test of low reliability could not possibly increase reliability—but it does. This example illustrates the great care needed in phrasing statements so that they are unequivocally true but do not contain "giveaways" to the answer.

4. Use negative statements sparingly and avoid double negatives.   The "no" or "not" in negative statements are frequently overlooked and they are read as positive statements. Thus, negative statements should be used only when the learning outcome requires it (e.g., in avoiding a harmful practice), and then the negative words should be emphasized by underlining or by use of capital letters.

Statements including double negatives tend to be so confusing that they should be restated in positive form.

Poor: *T F Correction-for-guessing is *not* a practice that should *never* be used in testing.

Better: *T F Correction-for-guessing is a practice that should sometimes be used in testing.

The double negatives in the "poor" version introduce sufficient ambiguity to cause the item to be a measure of reading comprehension. The "better" version clearly states the same idea in positive form.

5. Statements of opinion should be attributed to some source unless used to distinguish facts from opinion: A statement of opinion is not true or false by itself, and it is poor instructional practice to have students respond to it as if it were a factual statement. Obviously, the only way students could mark such an item correctly would be to agree with the opinion of the item writer. It is much more defensible to attribute the item to some source, such as an individual or organization. It then becomes a measure of how well the student knows the beliefs or values of that individual or organization.

Poor: T F Testing should play a major role in the teaching-learning process.

Better: *T F Gronlund believes that testing should play a major role in the teaching-learning process.

In some cases, it is useful to use a series of opinion statements that pertain to the same individual or organization. This permits a more comprehensive measure of how well the student understands a belief or value system.

Would the author of your textbook agree or disagree with the following statements? Circle A for agree, D for disagree.

  *A D 1. The first step in achievement testing is to state the intended learning outcomes in performance terms.

   A *D 2. True-false tests are superior to multiple-choice tests for measuring achievement.

Using about ten items like those listed here would provide a fairly good indication of the students' grasp of the author's point of view. Items like this are useful for measuring how well students understand a textbook without requiring them to agree with the opinions expressed. It is desirable, of course, to select opinion statements that are shared by many experts in the area.

Another valuable use of opinion statements is to ask students to distinguish between statements of fact and statements of opinion. This is an important outcome in its own right and is a basic part of critical thinking.

EXAMPLE

Read each of the following statements and circle F if it is a *fact* and circle O if it is an *opinion*.

```
*F    O   1.  The true-false item is a selection-type item.
 F   *O   2.  The true-false item is difficult to construct.
 F   *O   3.  The true-false item encourages student guessing.
*F    O   4.  The true-false item can be scored objectively.
```

In addition to illustrating the use of opinion statements in test items, the last two examples illustrate variations from the typical true-false format. These are more logically called *alternative-response* items.

6. When cause–effect relationships are being measured, use only true propositions.   The true-false item can be used to measure the "ability to identify cause–effect relationships" and this is an important aspect of understanding. When used for this purpose, both propositions should be true and only the relationship judged true or false.

EXAMPLE

Poor:	T *F	True-false items are classified as objective items	*because*	students must supply the answer.
Better:	T *F	True-false items are classified as objective items	*because*	there are only two possible answers.

The "poor" version is false because of the second part of the statement. With true-false items, students must *select* the answer rather than *supply* it. However, some students may mark this item false because they think the first part of the statement is incorrect. Thus, they receive one point because they *do not know* that true-false items are classified as objective items. Obviously, an item does not function as intended if misinformation can result in the correct answer. The problem with the "poor" version is that all three elements are permitted to vary (part one, part two, and the relationship between them) and it is impossible to tell what part the student is responding to when the item is marked false. In the "better" version both parts of the statement are true and the students must simply decide if the second part explains why the first part is true. In this case it does not, so it is marked false. Typically, a series of items like this is preceded by directions that make clear that only the relationship between the two parts of each statement is to be judged true or false.

7. Avoid extraneous clues to the answer. There are a number of *specific determiners* that provide verbal clues to the truth or falsity of an item. Statements that include such absolutes as "always," "never," "all," "none," and "only" tend to be false; statements with qualifiers such as "usually," "may," and "sometimes" tend to be true. Either these verbal clues must be eliminated from the statements, or their use must be balanced between true items and false items.

EXAMPLE

Poor:	T	*F	A statement of opinion should never be used in a true-false item.
Poor:	*T	F	A statement of opinion may be used in a true-false item.
Better:	*T	F	A statement of opinion, by itself, cannot be marked true or false.

The length and complexity of the statement might also provide a clue. True statements tend to be longer and more complex than false ones because of their need for qualifiers. Thus, a special effort should be made to equalize true and false statements in these respects.

A tendency to use a disproportionate number of true statements, or false statements, might also be detected and used as a clue. Having approximately, but not exactly, an equal number of each seems to be the best solution. When assembling the test, it is, of course, also necessary to avoid placing the correct answers in some discernible pattern (for instance, T, F, T, F). Random placement will eliminate this possible clue.

8. Base items on introductory material to measure more complex learning outcomes. True-false, or alternative-response items, are frequently used in interpreting written materials, tables, graphs, maps or pictures. The use of introductory material makes it possible to measure various types of complex learning outcomes. These item types will be illustrated in the section on interpretive exercises later in the chapter.

MATCHING ITEMS ✗ Could construct more than two columns

✗ appropriate

The matching item is simply a variation of the multiple-choice form. A good practice is to switch to the matching format only when it becomes apparent that the same alternatives are being repeated in several multiple-choice items.

EXAMPLE

Which test item is *least* useful for educational diagnosis?
   A.   Multiple-choice item.
  *B.   True-false item.
   C.   Short-answer item.

Which test item measures the greatest variety of learning outcomes?
  *A.   Multiple-choice item.
   B.   True-false item.
   C.   Short-answer item.
Which test item is difficult to score objectively?
   A.   Multiple-choice item.
   B.   True-false item.
  *C.   Short-answer item.
Which test item provides the highest score by guessing?
   A.   Multiple-choice item.
  *B.   True-False item.
   C.   Short-answer item.

By switching to a matching format we can eliminate the repetition of the alternative answers and present the same items in a more compact form. The matching format consists of a series of stems, called *premises*, and a series of alternative answers, called *responses*. These are arranged in columns with directions that set the rules for matching. The following example illustrates how our multiple-choice items can be converted to matching form.

EXAMPLE

Directions: Column A contains a list of characteristics of test items. On the line to the left of each statement, write the letter of the test item in Column B that best fits the statement. Each response in Column B may be used once, more than once, or not at all.

COLUMN A		COLUMN B
(B) 1. Least useful for educational diagnosis.		A. Multiple-choice item.
(A) 2. Measures greatest variety of learning outcomes.		B. True-false item.
(C) 3. Most difficult to score objectively.		C. Short-answer item.
(B) 4. Provides the highest score by guessing.		

The conversion to matching item illustrated here is probably the most defensible use of this item type. All too frequently, matching items consist of a disparate collection of premises, each of which has only one or two plausible answers. This can be avoided by starting with multiple-choice items and switching to the matching format only when it provides a more compact and efficient means of measuring the same achievement. In our example, we could have also expanded the item by adding other similar premises and responses.

Rules for Writing Matching Items

A good matching item should function the same as a series of multiple-choice items. As each premise is considered, all of the responses should serve as plausible alternatives. The rules for item writing are directed toward this end.

1. Include only homogeneous material in each matching item. In our earlier example of a matching item, we included *only* types of test items and their characteristics. Similarly, an item might include *only* authors and their works, inventors and their inventions, scientists and their discoveries, or historical events and their dates. This homogeneity is necessary if all responses are to serve as plausible alternatives.

2. Keep the lists of items short and place the brief responses on the right. A short list of items (say less than ten) will save reading time, make it easier for the student to locate the answer, and increase the likelihood that the responses will be homogeneous and plausible. Placing the brief responses on the right also saves reading time.

3. Use a larger, or smaller, number of responses than premises, and permit the responses to be used more than once. Both an uneven match and the possibility of using each response more than once reduces the guessing factor. As we noted earlier, proper use of the matching form requires that *all responses be plausible alternatives for each premise*. This, of course, dictates that each response be eligible for use more than once.

4. Specify in the directions the basis for matching, and indicate that each response may be used once, more than once, or not at all. This will clarify the task for all students and prevent any misunderstanding. Take care, however, not to make the directions too long and involved. The previous example illustrates adequate detail for directions.

5. Put all of the matching item on the same page. This will prevent the distraction of flipping pages back and forth, and prevent students from overlooking responses on another page.

THE INTERPRETIVE EXERCISE

Complex learning outcomes can frequently be more effectively measured by basing a series of test items upon a common selection of introductory material. This may be a paragraph, a table, a chart, a graph, a map, or a picture. The test items which follow the introductory material may be designed to call forth any type of intellectual ability or skill that can be measured objectively. This type of exercise is commonly called an *interpretive exercise* and both multiple-choice items and alternative-response items are widely used to measure interpretation of the introductory material.

The following example illustrates the use of multiple-choice items. Note that this item type makes it possible to measure a variety of learning outcomes with the same selection of introductory material. In this particular case, item 1 measures the *ability to recognize unstated assumptions*, item 2 the *ability to identify the meaning of a term*, and item 3 the *ability to identify relationships*.

EXAMPLE

Directions: Read the following comments a teacher made about testing. Then answer the questions that follow the comments by circling the letter of the best answer.

"Students go to school to learn, not to take tests. In addition, tests cannot be used to indicate a student's absolute level of learning. All tests can do is rank students in order of achievement, and this relative ranking is influenced by guessing, bluffing, and the subjective opinions of the teacher doing the scoring. The teaching-learning process would benefit if we did away with tests and depended on student self-evaluation."

1. Which one of the following unstated assumptions is this teacher making?
   A. Students go to school to learn.
   B. Teachers use essay tests primarily.
   *C. Tests make no contribution to learning.
   D. Tests do not indicate a student's absolute level of learning.

2. Which one of the following types of tests is this teacher primarily talking about?
   A. Diagnostic test.
   B. Formative test.
   C. Pretest.
   *D. Summative test.

3. Which one of the following propositions is most essential to the final conclusion?
   *A. Effective self-evaluation does not require the use of tests.
   B. Tests place students in rank order only.
   C. Tests scores are influenced by factors other than achievement.
   D. Students do not go to school to take tests.

The next example uses a modified version of the alternative-response form. This is frequently called a *key-type* item because a common set of alternatives is used in responding to each question. Note that the key-type item is devoted entirely to the measurement of one learning outcome. In this example the item measures the *ability to recognize warranted and unwarranted inferences*.

EXAMPLE

Directions: Paragraph A contains a description of the testing practices of Mr. Smith, a high school teacher. Read the description and each of the statements that follow it. Mark each statement to indicate the type of INFERENCE that can be drawn about it from the material in the paragraph. Place the appropriate letter in front of each statement using the following KEY:

   T—if the statement may be INFERRED as True.

   F—if the statement may be INFERRED as UNTRUE.

   N—if NO INFERENCE may be drawn about it from the paragraph.

PARAGRAPH A

Approximately one week before a test is to be given Mr. Smith carefully goes through the textbook and constructs multiple-choice items based on the material in the book. He always uses the exact wording of the textbook for the correct answer so that there will be no question concerning its correctness. He is careful to include some test items from each chapter. After the text is given, he lists the scores from high to low on the blackboard and tells each student his or her score. He does not return the test papers to the students, but he offers to answer any questions they might have about the test. He puts the items from each test into a test file, which he is building for future use.

STATEMENTS ON PARAGRAPH A

(T) 1. Mr. Smith's tests measure a limited range of learning outcomes.
(F) 2. Some of Mr. Smith's test items measure at the understanding level.
(N) 3. Mr. Smith's tests measure a balanced sample of subject-matter.
(N) 4. Mr. Smith uses the type of test item that is best for his purpose.
(T) 5. Students can determine where they rank in the distribution of scores on Mr. Smith's tests.
(F) 6. Mr. Smith's testing practices are likely to motivate students to overcome their weaknesses.

Key-type items are fairly easy to develop and can be directly related to specific learning outcomes. The key categories can, of course, be reused by simply changing the introductory material and the statements. Thus, they provide a standard framework for test preparation. Other common key categories include the following: (1) the argument is relevant, irrelevant, or neither; (2) the statement is supported by the evidence, refuted by the evidence, or neither; (3) the assumption is necessary or unnecessary; and (4) the conclusion is valid, invalid, or its validity cannot be determined. Although such standard key categories should not be applied in a perfunctory manner, they can provide guidelines to simplify the construction of the interpretive exercise.

Rules for Constructing Interpretive Exercises

The effectiveness of interpretive exercises, such as those illustrated earlier, depends on the care with which the introductory material is selected and the skill with which the dependent items are prepared. The following rules provide guidelines for preparing high quality exercises of this type.

1. Select introductory material that is relevant to the learning outcomes to be measured.   The introductory material may take many forms: written material, table, chart, graph, map, picture, or cartoon. In some cases the interpretation of the introductory material is an important learning outcome in its own right, as in the "interpretation of a weather map" or "the interpretation of a line graph." Here the nature of the introductory material is clearly prescribed by the intended outcome. In other cases, however, the introductory material simply provides the means for measuring other important outcomes. The "ability to distinguish between valid and invalid conclusions," for example, may be measured with different types of introductory material. In this instance we should select the type of material that provides the most direct measure of the learning outcome, is familiar to the examinees, and places the least demand on reading ability. For young children this means pictorial materials should typically be favored.

2. Select introductory material that is new to the examinees.   Although the form of the material should be familiar to the examinees, the specific content used in an exercise should be new to them. Thus, if they are asked to identify relationships shown in a graph, the type of graph should be familiar but the specific data in the graph must be new. If the data were the same as that presented in the classroom or described in the textbook, the exercise would measure nothing more than the simple recall of information. To measure complex outcomes, some novelty is necessary. How much depends on the specific nature of the intended outcome.

In some cases it is possible to locate introductory material that is new to the examinees by reviewing sources that are not readily available to them. Then it is simply a matter of adapting the material for testing purposes. In other cases it is necessary to prepare completely new material, that is, to write a paragraph, construct a graph, make a map, or draw a picture. In either case further revision will probably be needed when the dependent test items are being prepared. The process is essentially a circular one, with the writing of items requiring some changes in the introductory material and changes there providing ideas for new items. In carrying out this process of adapting and revising the material, be careful not to introduce so much novelty that the exercise no longer provides a valid measure of the intended learning outcome.

3. Keep the introductory material as brief as possible.   It is inefficient for both the test maker and the test taker to use extended introductory material and only one or two test items. If the introductory material is in written form, excessively long selections will also create problems for individuals with inadequate reading skills. Ideally we would like a brief, concise selection that contains enough ideas for several relevant test items. Material of this type can frequently be obtained from summaries, digests, and other condensed forms of written material. In some cases pictures or diagrams may provide the most concise summary of the material. As noted earlier we should always favor the type of material that places the least demand on reading ability.

4. Construct test items that call forth the type of performance specified in the learning outcome. To adequately measure the intended interpretation of the introductory material requires careful phrasing of the questions and special attention to two important cautions. First, *the answer to an item should not be given directly in the material* since some mental process beyond "recognition of a stated fact" is required in measures of intellectual skills. Second, *it should not be possible to answer the question without the introductory material.* If an item can be answered on the basis of general knowledge, it is not measuring the ability to interpret the material in the exercise. A good check on this type of error is to cover the introductory material and attempt to answer the questions without it.

5. Follow the rules of effective item writing that pertain to the type of objective item used. All of the rules for constructing the various types of objective test items discussed in the last two chapters are applicable to the construction of items used in interpretive exercises. Even greater care must be taken to avoid extraneous clues, however, since items in interpretive exercises seem especially prone to such clues and they tend to be more difficult to detect in these items. If the introductory material includes illustrations, for example, special attention should be directed to such things as the size, shape, and position of objects as possible extraneous clues. These are frequently overlooked by the test maker who is concentrating on the intricacies of the mental response required, but not by the unprepared student who is frantically searching for any solution to the problem.

The greatest help in constructing interpretive exercises is to review a wide range of sample exercises that use different types of introductory material and different forms of dependent test items. For locating illustrative exercises, see the list of references at the end of the chapter.[1]

SUMMARY OF POINTS

The emphasis in this chapter can be summarized by the following points.

1. A good practice is to start with multiple-choice items and switch to other selection-type items when more appropriate.
2. The true-false, or alternative-response, item is appropriate when there are only two possible alternatives.
3. The true-false item is used primarily to measure knowledge of specific facts, although there are some notable exceptions.

---

[1]See checklist in the appendix for reviewing true-false items, matching items, and the interpretive exercise.

4. Each true-false statement should contain only one central idea, be concisely stated, be free of clues and irrelevant sources of difficulty, and have an answer that experts would agree upon.

5. Modifications of the true-false item are especially useful for measuring the ability to "distinguish between fact and opinion" and "identify cause–effect relations."

6. Modifications of the true-false item can be used in interpretive exercises to measure various types of complex learning outcomes.

7. The matching item is a variation of the multiple-choice form and is appropriate when it provides a more compact and efficient means of measuring the same achievement.

8. The matching item consists of a list of *premises* and a list of the *responses* to be related to the premises.

9. A good matching item is based on homogeneous material, contains a brief list of premises and an uneven number of responses (more or less) that can be used more than once, and has the brief responses in the right-hand column.

10. The directions for a matching item should indicate the basis for matching and that each response can be used more than once.

11. The interpretive exercise consists of a series of selection-type items based on some type of introductory material (e.g., paragraph, table, chart, graph, map, or picture).

12. The interpretive exercise uses both multiple-choice and alternative-response items to measure a variety of complex learning outcomes.

13. The introductory material used in an interpretive exercise must be relevant to the outcomes to be measured, new to examinees, at the proper reading level, and as brief as possible.

14. The test items used in an interpretive exercise should call for the intended type of interpretation, and the answers to the items should be dependent on the introductory material.

15. The test items used in an interpretive exercise should be in harmony with the rules for constructing that item type.

ADDITIONAL READING

EBEL, R. L. AND D. A. FRISBIE, *Essentials of Educational Measurement*, 4th ed. (Englewood Cliffs, N.J.: Prentice-Hall, Inc., 1986). See Chapter 9, "True-False Test Items," for a more favorable treatment of this item type than that found in most educational measurement books.

EDUCATIONAL TESTING SERVICE, *Multiple Choice Questions: A Close Look* (Princeton, N.J.: Test Development Division, ETS, 1973). Illustrates the use of maps, graphs, diagrams, pictures, and written materials for measuring complex achievement.

GRONLUND, N. E., *Measurement and Evaluation in Teaching*, 5th ed. (New York: Macmillan Publishing Co., Inc., 1985). See Chapter 8, "Measuring Complex Achievement: The Interpretive Exercise," for a variety of illustrative exercises for different subject areas, grade levels, and types of introductory material.

MEHRENS, W. A., AND I. J. LEHMANN, *Measurement and Evaluation in Education and Psychology*, 3rd ed. (New York: Holt, Rinehart and Winston, Inc., 1984). See Chapter 7, "Writing Objective Test Items: The Multiple-Choice and Context-Dependent Items," for sample interpretive exercises and rules for writing them.

5

Constructing Supply Items

Short-answer and essay

For some learning outcomes it may be desirable to use supply-type items . . .
These include the ability to produce an answer . . . to create . . . to organize . . .
to integrate . . . to evaluate . . . and similar types of performance . . . Supply-
type items are classified by the length of response required—from a word,
number, or symbol to an extended discussion.

As noted in the last two chapters, selection-type items can be designed to measure a
variety of learning outcomes ranging from simple to complex. They tend to be
favored in achievement tests because they provide (1) greater control of the type of
response students can make, (2) broader sampling of achievement, and (3) quicker
and more objective scoring. Despite these advantages, supply-type items can also
play an important role in measuring achievement.

Supply-type items require students to produce the answer. This may be a
single word or a several page response. Although the length of response ranges
along a continuum, supply-type items are typically divided into (1) short-answer
items, (2) restricted-response essay, and (3) extended-response essay.

SHORT-ANSWER ITEMS

The short-answer (or completion) item requires the examinee to supply the appropriate words, numbers, or symbols to answer a question or complete a statement.

EXAMPLE

What are the incorrect responses in a multiple-choice item called? *(Distracters)*
The incorrect responses in a multiple-choice item are called *(distracters)*.

This item type also includes computational problems and any other simple item form that requires supplying the answer rather than selecting it. Except for its use in computational problems, the short-answer item is used primarily to measure simple knowledge outcomes.

The short-answer item appears to be easy to write and use but there are two major problems in constructing short-answer items. First, it is extremely difficult to phrase the question or incomplete statement so that only one answer is correct. In the example we have noted, for instance, a student might respond with any one of a number of answers that could be defended as appropriate. The student might write "incorrect alternatives," "wrong answers," "inappropriate options," "decoys," "foils," or some other equally decriptive response. Second, there is the problem of spelling. If credit is given only when the answer is spelled correctly, the poor spellers will be prevented from showing their true level of achievement and the test scores will become an uninterpretable mixture of knowledge and spelling skill. On the other hand, if attempts are made to ignore spelling during the scoring process, there is still the problem of deciding whether a badly spelled word represents the intended answer. This, of course, introduces an element of subjectivity which tends to make the scores less dependable as measures of achievement.

Due to these weaknesses, the short-answer item should be reserved for those special situations where supplying the answer is a necessary part of the learning outcome to be measured; for example, where the intent is to have students *recall* the information, where computational problems are used, or where a selection-type item would make the answer obvious. In these situations, the use of the short-answer item can be defended despite its shortcomings.

Rules for Writing Short-Answer Items

1. State the item so that only a single, brief answer is possible.   This requires great skill in phrasing and the use of precise terms. What appears to be a simple, clear question to the test maker can frequently be answered in many different ways, as we noted with the previous sample item. It helps to review the item with this rule in mind and revise as needed.

2. Start with a direct question and switch to an incomplete statement only when greater conciseness is possible by doing so.   The use of a direct question increases the likelihood that the problem will be stated clearly and that only one answer will be appropriate. Also, incomplete statements tend to be less ambiguous when they are based on problems that were first stated in question form.

EXAMPLE

What is another name for true-false items? *(alternative-response items)*
True-false items are also called *(alternative-response items)*.

In some cases, it is best to leave it in question form. This may make the item clearer, especially to younger students.

3. It is best to leave only one blank and it should relate to the main point of the statement. Leaving several blanks to be filled is often confusing and the answer to one blank may depend on the answer in another.

EXAMPLE

Poor: In terms of type of response, the *(matching)* item is most like the *(multiple-choice)* item.

Better: In terms of type of response, which item is most like the matching item? *(multiple-choice)*.

In the "poor" version, a number of different responses would have to be given credit, such as "short-answer" and "essay," and "true-false" and "multiple-choice." Obviously, the item would not function as originally intended.

It is also important to avoid asking students to respond to unimportant or minor aspects of a statement. Focus on the main idea of the item and leave a blank only for the key response.

4. Place the blanks at the end of the statement. This permits the student to read the complete problem before coming to the blank to be filled. With this procedure, confusion and rereading of the item is avoided and scoring is simplified. Constructing incomplete statements with blanks at the end is more easily accomplished when the item is first stated as a direct question, as suggested earlier. In some cases, it may be a matter of rewording the item and changing the response to be made.

EXAMPLE

Poor: *(Reliability)* is likely to increase when a test is lengthened.
Better: When a test is lengthened, reliability is likely to *(increase)*.

With this particular item, the "better" version also provides a more clearly focused item. The "poor" version could be answered by "validity," "time for testing," "fatigue," and other unintended but clearly correct responses. This again illustrates the great care needed in phrasing short-answer items.

5. Avoid extraneous clues to the answer.   One of the most common clues in short-answer items is the length of the blank. If a long blank is used for a long word and a short blank for a short word, this is obviously a clue. Thus, all blanks should be uniform in length. Another common clue is the use of the indefinite article "a" or "an" just before the blank. It sometimes gives away the answer, or at least rules out some possible incorrect answers.

EXAMPLE

> *Poor:*   The supply-type item used to measure the ability to organize and integrate material is called an *(essay item)*.
>
> *Better:*   Supply-type items used to measure the ability to organize and integrate material are called *(essay items)*.

The "poor" version rules out "short-answer item," the only other supply-type item, because it does not follow the article "an." One solution is to include both articles, using a(an). Another solution is to eliminate the article by switching to plural, as shown in the "better" version.

6. For numerical answers, indicate the degree of precision expected and the units in which they are to be expressed.   Indicating the degree of precision (e.g., to the nearest whole number) will clarify the task for students and prevent them from spending more time on an item than is required. Indicating the units in which to express the answer will aid scoring by providing a more uniform set of responses (e.g., minutes rather than fractions of an hour). When the learning outcome requires knowing the type of unit in common use and the degree of precision expected, this rule must then be disregarded.

ESSAY QUESTIONS

The most notable characteristic of the essay question is the freedom of response it provides. As with the short-answer item, students must produce their own answers. With the essay question, however, they are free to decide how to approach the problem, what factual information to use, how to organize the answer, and what degree of emphasis to give to each aspect of the response. Thus, the essay question is especially useful for measuring the ability to organize, integrate, and express ideas. These are the very types of performance for which selection-type items and short-answer items are so inadequate.

Despite the need for essay questions to measure the higher level learning outcomes, their usefulness is limited by several serious shortcomings.

1.   Sampling of achievement is inadequate because of the small number of questions that can be answered in the allotted testing time.
     Increase testing time.

2. Broad based essay questions are more difficult to relate to intended learning outcomes. *Construct the essay question w/ specifications for the expected answers.*

3. Writing skill influences the scoring. Skillful bluffing can raise scores, and errors in grammar and spelling typically lower scores. Poor handwriting also tends to lower scores.

4. Scoring essay answers is time consuming, subjective, and tends to be unreliable. *Depends on instructor — minimize the subjectivity — proper planning*

Because of these limitations essay questions are best reserved for those complex learning outcomes that cannot be measured by other means (e.g., the ability to organize, integrate and express ideas). These outcomes might also be measured by assigning out-of-class essays, giving students more time to both think and write.

In deciding when and how to use essay questions, it may be desirable to compare their relative merits with those of selection-type items as shown in Table 5.1. As can be seen in the table, both item types are efficient for certain purposes and inefficient for others. It is also apparent that the two types tend to complement each other in terms of the types of learning outcomes measured and the effect they are most likely to have on learning.

TABLE 5.1 Summary Comparison of Selection-Type Items and Essay Questions

	SELECTION-TYPE ITEMS	ESSAY QUESTIONS
Learning Outcomes Measured	Good for measuring outcomes at the knowledge, comprehension, and application levels of learning; inadequate for organizing and expressing ideas.	Inefficient for measuring knowledge outcomes; best for ability to organize, integrate and express ideas.
Sampling of Content	The use of a large number of items results in broad coverage which makes representative sampling of content feasible.	The use of a small number of items limits coverage which makes representative sampling of content infeasible.
Preparation of Items	Preparation of good items is difficult and time consuming.	Preparation of good items is difficult but easier than selection-type items.
Scoring	Objective, simple, and highly reliable.	Subjective, difficult, and less reliable.
Factors Distorting Scores	Reading ability and guessing.	Writing ability and bluffing.
Probable Effect on Learning	Encourages students to remember, interpret, and use the ideas of others.	Encourages students to organize, integrate, and express their own ideas.

Types of Essay Questions

The freedom of response permitted by essay questions varies considerably. Students may be required to give a brief and precise response, or they may be given great freedom in determining the form and scope of their answers. Questions of the first type are commonly called restricted-response questions and those of the second type are called extended-response questions. This is an arbitrary but convenient pair of categories for classifying essay questions.

Restricted-Response Questions   The restricted-response question places strict limits on the answer to be given. The boundaries of the subject matter to be considered are usually narrowly defined by the problem, and the specific form of the answer is also commonly indicated (by words such as "list," "define," and "give reasons"). In some cases the response is limited further by the use of introductory material or by the use of special directions:

EXAMPLE

Describe the relative merits of selection-type test items and essay questions for measuring learning outcomes at the comprehension level. Confine your answer to one page.

EXAMPLE

Mr. Rogers, a ninth-grade science teacher, wants to measure his students' "ability to interpret scientific data" with a paper-and-pencil test.
1. Describe the steps that Mr. Rogers should follow.
2. Give reasons to justify each step.

Restricting the form and scope of the answers to essay questions has both advantages and disadvantages. Such questions can be prepared more easily, related more directly to specific learning outcomes, and scored more easily. On the other hand, however, they provide little opportunity for the students to demonstrate their abilities to organize, to integrate, and to develop essentially new patterns of response. The imposed limitations make restricted-response items especially useful for measuring learning outcomes at the comprehension, application, and analysis levels of learning. They are of relatively little value for measuring outcomes at the synthesis and evaluation levels. At these levels the extended-response question provides the more appropriate measure.

Extended-Response Questions   The extended-response question gives the students almost unlimited freedom to determine the form and scope of their responses. Although in some instances rather rigid practical limits may be imposed, such as time limits or page limits, restrictions on the material to be included in the answer and on the form of the response are held to a minimum. The student must be given sufficient freedom to demonstrate skills of synthesis and evaluation, and just enough control to assure that the intended intellectual skills and abilities will be called forth by the question. Thus, the amount of structure will vary from item to item depending on the learning outcomes being measured, but the stress will always be on providing as much freedom as the situation permits.

EXAMPLE

Synthesis Outcome: For a course that you are teaching or expect to teach, prepare a complete plan for evaluating student achievement. Be sure to include the procedures you would follow, the instruments you would use, and the reasons for your choices.

EXAMPLE

Evaluation Outcome: (The student is given a complete achievement test that includes errors or flaws in the directions, in the test items, and in the arrangement of the items.) Write a critical evaluation of this test using as evaluative criteria the rules and standards for test construction described in your textbook. Include a detailed analysis of the test's strengths and weaknesses and an evaluation of its overall quality and probable effectiveness.

The extended-response question provides for the creative integration of ideas, the overall evaluation of materials, and a broad approach to problem solving. These are all important learning outcomes and ones that cannot be measured by other types of test items. The biggest problem, of course, is to evaluate the answers with sufficient reliability to provide a useful measure of learning. This is a difficult and time-consuming task, but the importance of the outcomes would seem to justify the additional care and effort required.

Rules for Writing Essay Questions

The construction of clear, unambiguous essay questions that call forth the desired responses is a much more difficult task than is commonly presumed. The following rules will not make the task any easier, but their application will result in essay items of higher quality.

1. Use essay questions to measure complex learning outcomes only. Most knowledge outcomes profit little from being measured by essay questions. These outcomes can usually be measured more effectively by objective items which lack the sampling and scoring problems that essay questions introduce. There may be a few exceptions, as when supplying the answer is a basic part of the learning outcome, but for most knowledge outcomes essay questions simply provide a less reliable measure with no compensating benefits.

At the comprehension, application, and analysis levels of learning, both objective tests and essay tests are useful. Even here, though, the objective test would seem to have priority, the essay test being reserved for those situations that require the student to *give* reasons, *explain* relationships, *describe* data, *formulate* conclusions, or in some other way produce the appropriate answer. Where supplying the answer is vital, a properly constructed restricted-response question is likely to be most appropriate.

At the synthesis and evaluation levels of learning, both the objective test and the restricted-response test have only limited value. These tests may be used to measure some specific aspects of the total process, but the production of a complete work (such as a plan of operation) or an overall evaluation of a work (for instance, an evaluation of a novel or an experiment) requires the use of extended-response questions. It is at this level that the essay form contributes most uniquely.

2. Relate the questions as directly as possible to the learning outcomes being measured.   Essay questions will not measure complex learning outcomes unless they are carefully constructed to do so. Each question should be specifically designed to measure one or more well-defined outcomes. Thus, the place to start, as is the case with objective items, is with a precise description of the performance to be measured. This will help determine both the content and form of the item and will aid in the phrasing of it.

The restricted-response item is related quite easily to a specific learning outcome because it is so highly structured. The limited response expected from the student also makes it possible for the test maker to phrase the question so that its intent is communicated clearly to the student. The extended-response item, however, requires greater freedom of response and typically involves a number of learning outcomes. This makes it more difficult to relate the question to the intended outcomes and to indicate the nature of the desired answer through the phrasing of the question. If the task is prescribed too rigidly in the question, the students' freedom to select, organize, and present the answer is apt to be infringed upon. One practical solution is to indicate to the students the criteria to be used in evaluating the answer. For example, a parenthetical statement such as the following might be added: "Your answer will be evaluated in terms of its comprehensiveness, the relevance of its arguments, the appropriateness of its examples, and the skill with which it is organized." This clarifies the task to the students without limiting their freedom, and makes the item easier to relate to clearly defined learning outcomes.

3. Formulate questions that present a clear task to be performed.   Phrasing an essay question so that the desired response is obtained is no simple matter. Selecting precise terms and carefully phrasing and rephrasing the question with the desired response in mind will help clarify the task to the student. Since essay questions are to be used as a measure of complex learning outcomes, avoid starting such questions with "who," "what," "when," "where," "name," and "list." These terms tend to limit the response to knowledge outcomes. Complex achievement is most apt to be called forth by such words as "why," "describe," "explain," "compare," "relate," "contrast," "interpret," "analyze," "criticize," and "evaluate." The specific terminology to be used will be determined largely by the specific behavior described in the learning outcome to be measured.

There is no better way to check on the phrasing of an essay question than to write a model answer, or at least to formulate a mental answer, to the question. This helps the test maker detect any ambiguity in the question, aids in determining the approximate time needed by the student to develop a satisfactory answer, and provides a rough check on the mental processes required. This procedure is most feasible with the restricted-response item, the answer to which is more limited and more closely prescribed. With the extended-response form it may be necessary to ask one or more colleagues to read the question to determine if the form and scope of the desired answer are clear.

4. Do not permit a choice of questions unless the learning outcome requires it.   In most tests of achievement, it is best to have all students answer the same questions. If they are permitted to write on only a fraction of the questions, such as three out of five, their answers cannot be evaluated on a comparative basis. Also, since the students will tend to choose those questions they are best prepared to answer, their responses will provide a sample of their achievement that is less representative than that obtained without optional questions. As we noted earlier, one of the major limitations of the essay test is the limited and unrepresentative sampling it provides. Giving students a choice among questions simply complicates the sampling problem further and introduces greater distortion into the test results.

In some situations the use of optional questions might be defensible. For example, if the essay is to be used as a measure of writing *skill* only, some choice of topics on which to write may be desirable. This might also be the case if the essay is used to measure some aspects of creativity, or if the students have pursued individual interests through independent study. Even for these special uses, however, great caution must be exercised in the use of optional questions. The ability to organize, integrate, and express ideas is determined in part by the complexity of the content involved. Thus, an indeterminate amount of contamination can be expected when optional questions are used.

5. Provide ample time for answering and suggest a time limit in each question.   Since essay questions are designed most frequently to measure intellectual skills and abilities, time must be allowed for thinking as well as for writing. Thus, generous time limits should be provided. For example, rather than expecting students to write on several essay questions during one class period, it might be better to have them focus on one or two. There seems to be a tendency for teachers to include so many questions in a single essay test that a high score is as much a measure of writing speed as of achievement. This is probably an attempt to overcome the problem of limited sampling, but it tends to be an undesirable solution. In measuring complex achievement, it is better to use fewer questions and to improve the sample by more frequent testing.

Informing students of the appropriate amount of time they should spend on each question will help them use their time more efficiently; ideally, it will also provide a more adequate sample of their achievement. If the length of the answer is not clearly defined by the problem, as in some extended-response questions, it might also be desirable to indicate page limits. Anything that will clarify the form and scope of the task without interfering with the measurement of the intended outcomes is likely to contribute to more effective measurement.

Rules for Scoring Essay Answers

As we noted earlier, one of the major limitations of the essay test is the subjectivity of the scoring. That is, the feelings of the scorers are likely to enter into the judgments they make concerning the quality of the answers. This may be a personal bias toward the writer of the essay, toward certain areas of content or styles of writing, or toward shortcomings in such extraneous areas as legibility, spelling, and grammar. These biases, of course, distort the results of a measure of achievement and tend to lower their reliability.

The following rules are designed to minimize the subjectivity of the scoring and to provide as uniform a standard of scoring from one student to another as possible. These rules will be most effective, of course, when the questions have been carefully prepared in accordance with the rules for construction.

1. Evaluate answers to essay questions in terms of the learning outcomes being measured.   The essay test, like the objective test, is used to obtain evidence concerning the extent to which clearly defined learning outcomes have been achieved. Thus, the desired student performance specified in these outcomes should serve as a guide both for constructing the questions and for evaluating the answers. If a question is designed to measure ''the ability to explain cause–effect relations,'' for example, the answer should be evaluated in terms of how adequately the student *explains the particular cause–effect relations presented in the question.* All other factors, such as interesting but extraneous factual information, style of writing, and errors in spelling and grammar, should be ignored (to the extent possible) during the evaluation. In some cases separate scores may be given for spelling or writing ability, but these should not be allowed to contaminate the scores that represent the degree of achievement of the intended learning outcomes.

2. Score restricted-response answers by the point method, using a model answer as a guide.   Scoring with the aid of a previously prepared scoring key is possible with the restricted-response item because of the limitations placed on the answer. The procedure involves writing a model answer to each question and determining the number of points to be assigned to it and to the parts within it. The distribution of points within an answer must, of course, take into account all scorable units indicated in the learning outcomes being measured. For example, points may be assigned to the relevance of the examples used and to the organization of the answer, as well as to the content of the answer, if these are legitimate aspects of the learning outcome. As indicated earlier, it is usually desirable to make clear to the student at the time of testing the bases on which each answer will be judged (content, organization, and so on).

3. Grade extended-response answers by the rating method, using defined criteria as a guide.   Extended-response items allow so much freedom in answering that the preparation of a model answer is frequently impossible. Thus, the test maker usually *grades* each answer by judging its quality in terms of a previously determined set of criteria, rather than *scoring* it point by point with a scoring key. The criteria for judging the quality of an answer are determined by the nature of the question and thus by the learning outcomes being measured. If students were asked to "describe a complete plan for preparing an achievement test," for example, the criteria would include such things as (1) the completeness of the plan (for example, whether it included a statement of objectives, a set of specifications, and the appropriate types of items, (2) the clarity and accuracy with which each step was described, (3) the adequacy of the justification for each step, and (4) the degree to which the various parts of the plan were properly integrated.

Typically the criteria for evaluating an answer are used to establish about five levels of quality. Then as the answer to a question is read, it is assigned a letter grade or a number from one to five, which designates the reader's rating. One grade may be assigned on the basis of the overall quality of the answer, or a separate judgment may be made on the basis of each criterion. The latter procedure provides the most useful information for diagnosing and improving learning and should be used wherever possible.

More uniform standards of grading can usually be obtained by reading the answers to each question twice. During the first reading the papers should be tentatively sorted into five piles, ranging from high to low in quality. The second reading can then serve the purpose of checking the uniformity of the answers in each pile and making any necessary shifts in rating.

4. Evaluate all of the students' answers to one question before proceeding to the next question.   Scoring or grading essay tests question by question, rather than student by student, makes it possible to maintain a more uniform standard for judging the answers to each question. This procedure also helps offset the *halo effect* in grading. When all of the answers on one paper are read together, the grader's impression of the paper as a whole is apt to influence the grades assigned to the individual answers. Grading question by question prevents the formation of this overall impression of a student's paper. Each answer is more apt to be judged on its own merits when it is read and compared with other answers to the same question than when it is read and compared with other answers by the same student.

5. Evaluate answers to essay questions without knowing the identity of the writer.   This is another attempt to control personal bias during scoring. Answers to essay questions should be evaluated in terms of what is written, not in terms of what is known about the writers from other contacts with them. The best way to prevent prior knowledge from biasing our judgment is to evaluate each answer without knowing the identity of the writer. This can be done by having the students write their names on the back of the paper or by using code numbers in place of names.

6. Whenever possible, have two or more persons grade each answer.   The best way to check on the reliability of the scoring of essay answers is to obtain two or more independent judgments. Although this may not be a feasible practice for routine classroom testing, it might be done periodically with a fellow teacher (one who is equally competent in the area). Obtaining two or more independent ratings becomes especially vital where the results are to be used for important and irreversible decisions,such as in the selection of students for further training or for special awards. Here, the pooled ratings of several competent persons may be needed to attain a level of reliability that is commensurate with the significance of the decision being made.[1]

SUMMARY OF POINTS

The emphasis in this chapter can be summarized by the following points.

1.   Use supply-type items whenever producing the answer is an essential element in the learning outcome (e.g., *defines* terms, instead of *identifies* meaning of terms).
2.   Supply-type items include short-answer items, restricted-response essay, and extended-response essay.
3.   The short-answer item can be answered by a word, number, symbol, or brief phrase.
4.   The short-answer item is limited primarily to measuring simple knowledge outcomes.
5.   Each short-answer item should be so carefully written that there is only one possible answer, the entire item can be read before coming to the answer space, and there are no extraneous clues to the answer.
6.   In scoring short-answer items, give credit for all correct answers and score for spelling separately.
7.   Essay questions are most useful for measuring the ability to organize, integrate, and express ideas .
8.   Essay questions are inefficient for measuring knowledge outcomes because they provide limited sampling, are influenced by extraneous factors (e.g., writing skills, bluffing, grammar, spelling, handwriting), and scoring is subjective and unreliable.
9.   Restricted-response essay questions can be more easily written and scored but due to limitations on the responses are less useful for measuring the higher level outcomes (e.g., integration of diverse material).

[1]See checklist in Appendix for reviewing short-answer items and essay items.

10. Extended-response essay questions give students the freedom to select, organize, and express ideas in the manner they think is most appropriate and are, therefore, especially useful for measuring such outcomes.

11. Essay questions should be written in such a way that they present a clear task and contain only those restrictions needed to call forth the intended response and provide for adequate scoring.

12. Essay answers should be scored by focusing on the intended response, by using a model answer or set of criteria as a guide, by scoring question by question, and by ignoring the writer's identity. If an important decision is to be based on the results, two or more competent scorers should be used.

ADDITIONAL READING

EBEL, R. L., AND D. A. FRISBIE, *Essentials of Educational Measurement,* 4th ed. (Englewood Cliffs, N.J.: Prentice-Hall, Inc., 1986). See Chapter 8, "The Use of Essay Tests," for a comparison with objective tests and guidelines for preparing essay items.

GRONLUND, N. E., *Measurement and Evaluation in Teaching,* 5th ed. (New York: Macmillan Publishing Co., Inc., 1985). See Chapter 9, "Measuring Complex Achievement: The Essay Test," for a comparison of the essay test to the interpretive exercise and illustrative thought questions for use in essay tests.

HOPKINS, K. D., AND J. C. STANLEY, *Educational and Psychological Measurement and Evaluation,* 6th ed. (Englewood Cliffs, N.J.: Prentice-Hall, Inc., 1981). See Chapter 8, "Constructing and Using Essay Tests," for a discussion of the limitations of essay tests and methods of improving their construction and use.

MEHRENS, W. A., AND I. J. LEHMANN, *Measurement and Evaluation in Education and Psychology,* 3rd ed. (New York: Holt, Rinehart & Winston, Inc., 1984). See Chapter 5, "The Essay Test: Preparing the Questions and Grading the Responses," for examples of essay questions and rules for constructing and scoring.

6

Constructing Performance Tests

Performance tests are useful in a variety of instructional areas. . . . These tests vary from paper-and-pencil measures of performance to samples of actual job performance. . . . As with other test types, the nature of the performance test is determined primarily by the instructional outcomes to be measured . . . and the quality of the test is enhanced by following a systematic procedure of test development.

Performance tests are concerned with skill outcomes. Skill in using processes and procedures is a desired outcome in many academic courses. For example, science courses are typically concerned with laboratory skills, mathematics courses are concerned with practical problem-solving skills, English and foreign language courses are concerned with communication skills, and social studies courses are concerned with such skills as map and graph construction and operating effectively in a group. In addition, skill outcomes are emphasized heavily in art and music courses, industrial education, business education, agricultural education, home economics courses, and physical education. Thus, in most instructional areas performance testing provides a useful adjunct to the more commonly used paper-and-pencil measures of knowledge. Although measures of knowledge can tell us whether students know what to do in a particular situation, performance tests are needed to assess their actual performance skills.

Performance testing, despite the need for it, is frequently neglected in the measurement of instructional outcomes. There may be many reasons for this, but two are readily apparent. First, performance tests are more difficult to use than knowledge tests. They typically require more time to prepare and administer, and scoring them is frequently subjective and burdensome. Second, our past emphasis on norm-referenced measurement has made indirect measurement acceptable. Thus, if it could be shown that "knowledge about" an activity was related to actual performance of the activity, the more convenient knowledge measure could be substituted for the performance measure (since both would rank students in approximately the same order). The acceptability of such indirect measurement in education has led to an overemphasis on "knowing about" and an underemphasis on "skill in doing." The advent of criterion-referenced measurement which emphasizes describing specifically *what each individual can and cannot do* has put things back in proper perspective. With this form of measurement, if you want to determine what an individual "knows about" a given performance, a knowledge test is perfectly appropriate. However, if you want to describe "proficiency in performing an activity," a performance test must be used. No matter how highly related the results of the two types of test might be, the scores on the knowledge test obviously cannot be used to describe an individual's performance skills. This emphasis on measuring each instructional outcome as directly as possible for descriptive purposes can be expected to give performance testing a much more prominent place in educational measurement.

THE NATURE OF PERFORMANCE TESTING

A performance test typically falls somewhere between the usual paper-and-pencil test of cognitive outcomes and performance in the natural situation in which the learning is ultimately to be applied. As Fitzpatrick and Morrison (1971) indicate, the simulation of the "real-life situation" is a matter of degree and, thus, we can expect performance tests in any particular area to vary in the amount of "realism" that is incorporated into the test situation.

The presence of varying degrees of realism in performance testing can be illustrated by the simple example of applying arithmetic skills to the practical problem of determining correct change while shopping in a store (adapted from Fitzpatrick and Morrison, 1971). A simulation of this situation might range from the use of a story problem (low realism) to an actual purchase in a storelike situation (high realism). The various problem situations that might be contrived for this performance measure are shown in Figure 6.1. It should be noted that even though solving a story problem is relatively low in realism, it simulates the criterion situation to a greater degree than simply asking students to subtract 69 from 100. Thus, even in paper-and-pencil testing it is frequently possible to increase the degree of realism to a point where the results are useful in assessing performance outcomes.

As we shall see later, the degree of realism to be incorporated into a performance situation depends on the purpose of the instruction, the location of the performance assesment in the instructional sequence, the practical constraints operating (such as time, cost and availability of equipment), and the nature of the particular task being measured. We shall always favor the performance measure with the

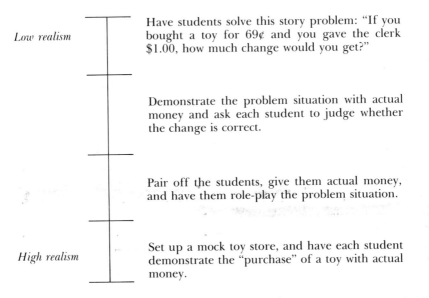

Low realism

Have students solve this story problem: "If you bought a toy for 69¢ and you gave the clerk $1.00, how much change would you get?"

Demonstrate the problem situation with actual money and ask each student to judge whether the change is correct.

Pair off the students, give them actual money, and have them role-play the problem situation.

High realism

Set up a mock toy store, and have each student demonstrate the "purchase" of a toy with actual money.

FIGURE 6.1.   Illustration of Various Degrees of Realism in Measuring the Ability to Determine Correct Change while Making a Purchase in a Store.

highest degree of realism, but these numerous mediating factors may force us to settle for a degree of realism that falls far short of the ideal.

Procedure Versus Product

Performance testing focuses on the procedure, the product, or some combination of the two. The nature of the performance frequently dictates where the emphasis should be placed.

Some types of performance do not result in a tangible product. Typical examples of such performance include manipulating laboratory equipment, making a speech, playing a musical instrument, and various physical feats (for instance, swimming, dancing, and throwing a ball). Activities such as these require that the performance be evaluated in progress, special attention being paid to the constituent movements and their proper sequencing.

In some areas of performance, the product is the focus of attention and the procedure (or process) is of little or no significance. In evaluating a student's theme, drawing, or insect display, for example, the teacher is not likely to assess the procedures used by the student. This might be because various procedures could lead to an equally good product, or because the product was the result of a take-home project and the process was therefore not observable by the teacher. Also, some in-class activities are nonobservable because they involve primarily mental processes (such as problem-solving skills). In any event, in some cases only the product is evaluated. Judging the quality of the product is typically guided by specific criteria that have been prepared especially for that purpose.

In many cases both procedure and product are important aspects of a performance. For example, skill in locating and correcting a malfunction in a television set involves following a systematic procedure (rather than using trial and error) in addition to producing a properly repaired set. Frequently procedure is emphasized during the early stages of learning and products later, after the procedural steps have been mastered. In assessing typing skills, for example, proper use of the "touch system" would be evaluated at the beginning of instruction, but later evaluation would focus on the neatness and accuracy of the typed material and the speed with which it was produced. Similarly in such areas as cooking, woodworking, and painting, correct procedure is likely to be stressed during the early stages of instruction and the quality of the product later. Thus, where both the procedure and the product of a performance skill are important, the degree of emphasis given to each in the assessment depends on both the skill being measured and the position of the task in the instructional sequence.

TYPES OF PERFORMANCE TESTS

Performance tests can be classified in various ways. A classification system that roughly approximates the degree of realism present in the test situation includes the following types: (1) paper-and-pencil performance, (2) identification test, (3) simulated performance, and (4) work sample. Although these categories overlap to some degree, they provide a useful means of describing various approaches that might be used in measuring applied performance skills. In some cases only one of the approaches might be used in measuring a particular skill. More commonly two or more approaches are likely to be used at different stages of instruction.

Paper-and-Pencil Performance

A paper-and-pencil performance test differs from the more traditional paper-and-pencil test by placing greater emphasis on the application of knowledge and skill in a simulated setting. These paper-and-pencil applications might result in desired terminal learning outcomes, or they might serve as an intermediate step to performance that involves a higher degree of realism (for example, the actual use of equipment).

In a number of instances, paper-and-pencil performance can provide a product of educational significance. A course in test construction, for example, might require students to perform activities such as the following:

Construct a set of test specifications for a unit of instruction.
Construct a set of test items that fits a given set of specifications.
Construct a checklist for evaluating an achievement test.

The action verb *construct* is frequently used in paper-and-pencil performance testing. For instance, students might be asked to construct a weather map, bar graph, diagram of an electrical circuit, floor plan, design for an article of clothing, poem, short story, or plan for an experiment. In such cases, the paper-and-pencil product is a result of both knowledge and skill, and it provides a performance measure that is valued in its own right.

In other cases paper-and-pencil performance might simply provide a first step toward "hands-on" performance. For example, before using a particular measuring instrument, such as a micrometer, it might be desirable to have students read various settings from pictures of the scale. Although the ability to read the scale is not a sufficient condition for accurate measurement, it is a necessary one. In this instance, paper-and-pencil testing would be favored because it is a more convenient method of testing a group of students. Using paper-and-pencil performance tests as a precursor to "hands-on" performance might be favored for other reasons. For example, if the performance is complicated and the equipment is expensive, demonstrating competence in paper-and-pencil situations could avoid subsequent accidents or damage to equipment. Similarly in the health sciences, skill in diagnosing and prescribing for hypothetical patients could avoid later harm to real patients.

Identification Test

The identification test includes a wide variety of test situations representing various degrees of realism. In some cases a student may be asked simply to identify a tool or piece of equipment and to indicate its function. A more complex test situation might present the students with a particular performance task (for example, locating a short in an electrical circuit) and ask them to identify the tools, equipment, and procedures needed in performing the task. An even more complex type of identification test might involve listening to the operation of a malfunctioning machine (such as an automobile motor, a drill, or a lathe) and, from the sound, identifying the most probable cause of the malfunction and the proper procedure for correcting it.

Although identification tests are widely used in industrial education, they are by no means limited to that area. The biology teacher might have students identify specimens that are placed at various stations around the room, or identify the equipment and procedures needed to conduct a particular experiment. Similarly chemistry students might be asked to identify "unknown" substances, foreign language students to identify correct pronunciation, mathematics students to identify correct problem-solving procedures, English students to identify the "best expression" to be used in writing, and social studies students to identify various leadership roles as they are "acted out" in a group. Identifying correct procedures is also important, of course, in art, music, physical education, and such vocational areas as agriculture, business education, and home economics.

The identification test is sometimes used as an indirect measure of performance skill. The experienced plumber, for example, is expected to have a broader knowledge of tools and equipment used in plumbing than the inexperienced plumber. Thus, a tool identification test might be used to eliminate the least skilled in a group of applicants for a position as plumber. More commonly the identification test is used as an instructional device to prepare students for actual performance in real or simulated situations.

Simulated Performance

Simulated performance emphasizes proper procedure. The student is typically expected to perform the same motions as those required in the actual performance of the task, but the conditions are simulated. In physical education, for example, swinging a bat at an imaginary ball, shadow boxing, and demonstrating various swimming strokes out of water are simulated performances. In science and vocational courses, laboratory work is frequently designed to simulate actual job performance. Similarly in social studies, student role-playing of a jury trial, a city council meeting, or a job interview provides the instructor with opportunities to measure the simulated performance of an assigned task. In some cases, specially designed equipment is used for instructional and evaluative purposes. In both driver training and flight training, for example, students are frequently trained and tested on simulators. Such simulators may prevent personal injury or damage to expensive equipment during the early stages of skill development. Simulators are also used in various types of vocational training programs.

In some situations, simulated performance testing might be used as the final assessment of a performance skill. This would be the case in assessing students' laboratory performance in chemistry, for example. In many situations, however, skill in a simulated setting simply indicates readiness to attempt actual performance. The student in driver training who has demonstrated driving skill in the simulator, for example, is now ready to apply this skill in the actual operation of an automobile.

Work Sample

Of the various types of performance tests, the work sample incorporates the highest degree of realism. It requires the student to perform actual tasks that are representative of the total performance to be measured. The sample tasks typically include the most crucial elements of the total performance and are performed under controlled conditions. In being tested for automobile driving skill, for example, the student is required to drive over a standard course that includes the most common problem situations likely to be encountered in normal driving. Each student's performance on the standard course is then used as evidence of that individual's ability to drive an automobile under typical operating conditions.

Performance tests in business education and industrial education are frequently of the work-sample type. When students are required to take and transcribe shorthand notes from dictation, type a business letter, or operate a key punch in processing business data, a work-sample assessment is being employed. Similarly in industrial education, a work-sample approach is being used when students are required to complete a metalworking or woodworking project that includes all of the steps likely to be encountered in an actual job situation (steps such as designing, ordering materials, and constructing). Still other examples are the operation of machinery, the repair of equipment, and the performance of job-oriented laboratory tasks. The work-sample approach to assessing performance is widely used in occupations involving performance skills, and many of these situations can be duplicated in the school setting.

STEPS IN CONSTRUCTING A PERFORMANCE TEST

Construction of a performance test follows somewhat the same pattern used in constructing other types of achievement tests but involves some added complexities. The test situations can seldom be fully controlled and standardized, they typically take more time to prepare and administer, and they are frequently more difficult to score. In general the closer the test situation approximates actual performance conditions, the greater the problems encountered in the assessment. The following procedural steps are ways of dealing with some of the common problems to be encountered in the development of performance tests. More elaborate descriptions can be found in Boyd and Shimberg (1971) and Fitzpatrick and Morrison (1971).

1. Specify the performance outcomes to be measured.   If the objectives of the instruction have been prespecified, the problem is simply to select those that require the use of performance tests. If the objectives have not been prespecified, they should be identified and defined for the particular areas of performance to be measured. Performance objectives commonly use action verbs such as *identify*, *construct*, and *demonstrate* (and their synonyms). A brief description of these verbs and illustrative objectives is shown in Table 6.1. Most of these sample objectives would have to be defined further by a set of specific learning outcomes, following the procedure described in Chapter 2.

The specification of intended outcomes for performance testing typically includes a job or task analysis that identifies the specific activities that are most critical in successful performance. Since it is frequently impossible to measure all the procedures involved in a particular task, it is necessary to focus on a representative sample of the most crucial ones. In addition to being representative of the total performance, the selected activities should, of course, also reflect the emphasis given during instruction and should be measurable.

When the critical elements of the performance have been identified and specified, it may be desirable to set performance standards for each task. These standards indicate the minimum level of performance that is considered acceptable. They might be concerned with the accuracy of the performance (for example, "measures temperature *to the nearest two tenths of a degree*"), the speed of the performance ("locate a malfunction in electronic equipment *within three minutes*"), the proper sequencing of the steps ("adjusts a microscope *following the proper sequence of steps*"), or some subjective quality ("handles tools and equipment *skillfully*"). In the last case the subjective quality "skillfully" would have to be defined further so that observers could agree on what constitutes a minimum level of skill. The various standards set may, of course, be combined in one criterion of successful performance. In the case of the oral thermometer, for exam-

TABLE 6.1   Typical Action Verbs and Illustrative Instructional Objectives for Performance Outcomes

ACTION VERBS	ILLUSTRATIVE INSTRUCTIONAL OBJECTIVES
IDENTIFY: selects the correct objects, part of the object, procedure, or property (*typical verbs:* identify, locate, select, touch, pick up, mark, describe)	Select the proper tool. Identify the parts of a typewriter. Choose correct laboratory equipment. Select the most relevant statistical procedure. Locate an automobile malfunction. Identify a musical selection. Identify the experimental equipment needed. Identify a specimen under the microscope.
CONSTRUCT: make a product to fit a given set of specifications (*typical verbs:* construct, assemble, build, design, draw, make, prepare)	Draw a diagram for an electrical circuit. Design a pattern for making a dress. Assemble equipment for an experimental study. Prepare a circle graph. Construct a weather map. Prepare an experimental design. Build a coffee table.
DEMONSTRATE: performs a set of operations or procedures (*typical verbs:* demonstrate, drive, measure, operate, perform, repair, set up)	Drive an automobile. Measure the volume of a liquid. Operate a filmstrip projector. Perform a modern dance step. Repair a malfunctioning TV set. Set up laboratory equipment. Demonstrate taking a patient's temperature. Demonstrate the procedure for tuning an automobile.

ple, one criterion would typically specify both the proper procedures and the accuracy of measurement. Similarly many performance skills combine standards of speed and accuracy (for instance, ''types fifty words per minute with a maximum of two errors''). See the accompanying box for some commonly used standards.

The importance to be assigned to each dimension of successful performance depends on the stage of instruction as well as on the nature of the performance. In assessing laboratory measurement skills, for example, accuracy might be stressed early in the instruction, and concern about speed of performance might be delayed until the later stages of instruction. The particular situation in which the task is to be performed may also influence the importance of each dimension. In the measurement of typing skill, for example, speed might be stressed in the typing of routine business letters, whereas accuracy would be emphasized in the tying of statistical tables for economic reports.

2. Select an appropriate degree of realism.   The degree of realism selected for a particular test situation depends on a number of factors. First, the nature of the instructional objectives must be considered. Acceptable performance in paper-and-

SOME COMMON STANDARDS FOR JUDGING PERFORMANCE	
TYPE	EXAMPLES
Rate	Solve ten addition problems in two minutes. Type 40 words per minute.
Error	No more than two errors per typed page. Count to 20 in Spanish without error.
Time	Set up laboratory equipment in five minutes. Locate an equipment malfunction in three minutes.
Precision	Measure a line within one eighth of an inch. Read a thermometer within two tenths of a degree.
Quantity	Complete 20 laboratory experiments. Locate 15 relevant references.
Quality (rating)	Write a neat, well-spaced business letter. Demonstrate correct form in diving.
Percentage Correct	Solve 85 percent of the math problems. Spell correctly 90 percent of the words in the word list.
Steps Required	Diagnose a motor malfunction in five steps. Locate a computer error using proper sequence of steps.
Use of Material	Build a bookcase with less than 10 percent waste. Cut out a dress pattern with less than 10 percent waste.
Safety	Check all safety guards before operating machine. Drive automobile without breaking any safety rules.

pencil applications of skill, or in other measures with a low degree of realism, might be all that the instruction is intended to achieve. This is frequently the case with introductory courses that are to be followed by more advanced courses emphasizing applied performance. Second, the sequence of instruction within a particular course may indicate that it would be desirable to measure paper-and-pencil applications before "hands-on" performance is attempted. Locating the source of a malfunction on a diagram, for example, might precede working with actual equipment. Third, numerous practical constraints, such as time, cost, availability of equipment, and difficulties in administering and scoring, may limit the degree of realism that can be obtained. Fourth, the task may restrict the degree of realism in a test situation. In testing first aid skills, for example, it would be infeasible (and undesirable) to use actual patients with the wounds, broken bones, and other physical conditions needed for testing. Thus, although we should strive for as high a degree of realism as the performance outcomes dictate, it is frequently necessary to make compromises in preparing test situations.

3. Prepare instructions that clearly specify the test situation.   When the test situation has been selected and the specific tasks to be performed have been identified, the next step is to prepare instructions that clearly describe the test situation. These instructions should describe the required performance and the conditions under which the performance is to be demonstrated. Instructions for a work-sample test typically include the following points:

A.   purpose of the test
B.   equipment and materials
C.   testing procedure:
    (1)   condition of equipment
    (2)   required performance
    (3)   time limits (if any)
D.   method of scoring

The instructions are usually written so that all individuals are presented with the same task. In some cases the instructions are read to the examinees, and in others they read them themselves. The method of presentation depends on the complexity of the instructions and the reading ability of the examinees. In any event the method of presentation should be specified and should be the same for all examinees.

Carefully specifying what the examinees are to do, the conditions under which they are to perform, and the basis on which their performances are to be judged increases the likelihood that the test situation will be standard for all individuals.

4. Prepare the observational form to be used in evaluating performance.   As we noted earlier, the evaluation of performance focuses on the procedure, the product, or some combination of the two. Procedures and products are frequently evaluated by some type of checklist or rating scale. In addition products are sometimes evaluated by means of a "product scale." Each of these will be described.

The *product scale* is a series of sample products that reflect different degrees of quality. A scale of this type is useful in judging the overall quality of a product and is commonly used in evaluating handwriting, works of art, and vocational projects of various types. The procedure involves selecting sample products (for instance, those of students) representing five to seven levels of quality, arranging them in order of merit, and then assigning numerical values to the levels (for example, 1 to 7). Each student's product is then rated by comparing it to the scale and determining which quality level it matches most closely. A product scale is especially useful if the quality of the product being assessed is difficult to define by a set of separate dimensions, as is the case with paintings, handicrafts, and similar works of art.

The *checklist* is basically a list of measurable dimensions of a performance or product with a place to record a simple "yes" or "no" judgment. If a checklist were used to evaluate a set of procedures, for example, the steps to be followed might be placed in sequential order on the form; the observer would then simply check whether each action was taken or not taken. Such a checklist for evaluating the proper use of an oral thermometer is shown in Figure 6.2. A checklist for evaluating a product typically contains a list of the dimensions that characterize a good product (such as size, color, and shape), and a place to check whether each desired characteristic is present or absent.

The *rating scale* is similar to the checklist, but instead of a simple "yes" or "no" response it provides an opportunity to mark the degree to which each dimension is present. The rating scale can also be used for both procedures and products, as illustrated in the rating scale for a woodworking project shown in Figure 6.3. Although this numerical rating scale uses fixed alternatives ("outstanding," "above average"), rating scales frequently use separate descriptive phrases for each of the dimensions to be rated (see Gronlund, 1985). Like the checklist, the rating scale is a means of judging all students on the same set of dimensions, and it provides a convenient form on which to record the judgments. The type of observation method used will depend mainly on the nature of the performance being evaluated.

FIGURE 6.2. Checklist for Evaluating the Proper Use of an Oral Thermometer.

DIRECTIONS: Place a check in front of each step as it is performed

_____   1. Removes thermometer from container by grasping nonbulb end.

_____   2. Wipes thermometer downward from nonbulb end with fresh wiper.

_____   3. Shakes thermometer down to less than 96° while holding nonbulb end.

_____   4. Places bulb end of thermometer under patient's tongue.

_____   5. Tells patient to close lips but to avoid biting on thermometer.

_____   6. Leaves thermometer in patient's mouth for three minutes.

_____   7. Removes thermometer from patient's mouth by grasping nonbulb end.

_____   8. Reads temperature to the nearest *two tenths* of a degree.

_____   9. Records temperature reading on patient's chart.

_____   10. Cleans thermometer and replaces in container.

DIRECTIONS: Rate each of the following items by circling the appropriate number. The numbers represent the following values: 5–outstanding; 4–above average; 3–average; 2–below average; 1–unsatisfactory.

Procedure Rating Scale

How effective was the student's performance in each of the following areas?

5 4 3 2 1 (a) Preparing a detailed plan for the project.
5 4 3 2 1 (b) Determining the amount of material needed.
5 4 3 2 1 (c) Selecting the proper tools.
5 4 3 2 1 (d) Following the correct procedures for each operation.
5 4 3 2 1 (e) Using tools properly and skillfully.
5 4 3 2 1 (f) Using materials without unnecessary spoilage.
5 4 3 2 1 (g) Completing the work within a reasonable amount of time.

Product Rating Scale

To what extent does the product meet the following criteria?

5 4 3 2 1 (a) The product appears neat and well constructed.
5 4 3 2 1 (b) The dimensions match the original plan.
5 4 3 2 1 (c) The finish meets specifications.
5 4 3 2 1 (d) The joints and parts fit properly.
5 4 3 2 1 (e) The materials were used effectively.

FIGURE 6.3.   Rating Scale for a Woodworking Project.

SUMMARY OF POINTS

The emphasis in this chapter can be summarized by the following points.

1. Performance tests are useful for measuring various skills in academic courses (e.g., communication, laboratory, and problem-solving skills) and are of major importance for measuring learning outcomes in art, music, physical education, and vocational courses.
2. Performance testing emphasizes "skill in doing" rather than "knowing about" an activity.
3. There are varying degrees of realism in performance testing, and the aim is to obtain as high a degree of realism as possible within the various constraints operating (e.g., time, cost, availability of equipment).
4. Performance testing may focus on a procedure (e.g., giving a speech), a product (e.g., a theme), or both (e.g., uses tools properly in building a bookcase).

5. In some cases, it may be desirable to emphasize procedure evaluation during the early stages of instruction (e.g., touch system in typing) and product evaluation later (typed letter).

6. Paper-and-pencil performance testing is useful as a terminal measure in many areas (e.g., writing, drawing, problem solving) and can serve as a first step toward "hands-on" performance in others (e.g., procedure for providing an automobile engine tune-up).

7. The identification test is typically concerned with identifying the tools, equipment, and procedures needed for a performance task and serves as an indirect measure of performance skill, or as an instructional device to prepare students for actual performance.

8. Performance testing based on simulated performance (e.g., driver's training simulator) and the work sample (e.g., process business data on a computer) has the highest degree of realism. Many performance skills in laboratory courses, busines education and industrial education can be evaluated at this level.

9. The steps in constructing a performance test include specifying the outcomes to be measured, selecting an appropriate degree of realism, preparing a clear set of instructions, and preparing the evaluation form to be used.

10. The product scale (a graded set of products), checklist, and rating scale are the most commonly used forms of evaluation.

ADDITIONAL READING

BALDWIN, T. S., "Evaluation of Learning in Industrial Education," Chapter 23 in B. S. Bloom, J. T. Hastings, and G. F. Madaus, *Handbook on Formative and Summative Evaluation of Student Learning* (New York: McGraw-Hill Book Company, 1971). Includes illustrative tables of specifications and test items.

BOYD, J. L., AND B. SHIMBERG, *Handbook of Performance Testing: A Practical Guide for Test Makers* (Princeton, N.J.: Educational Testing Service, 1971). Describes how to prepare performance measures and presents a portfolio of sample performance tests.

FITZPATRICK, R., AND E. J. MORRISON, "Performance and Product Evaluation," Chapter 9 in R. L. Thorndike, ed., *Educational Measurement*, 2nd ed. (Washington, D.C.: American Council on Education, 1971). A comprehensive discussion of the principles and procedures of performance testing.

GRONLUND, N. E., *Measurement and Evaluation in Teaching*, 5th ed. (New York: Macmillan Publishing Co., Inc., 1985). Chapter 15, "Evaluating Learning and Development: Observational Techniques." Describes the preparation and use of anecdotal records, rating scales, and checklists.

PRIESTLY, M., *Performance Assessment in Education and Training: Alternative Techniques* (Englewood Cliffs, N.J.: Educational Technology Publications, 1982). A treatment of 25 types of performance assessment. Includes test development and use.

STIGGINS, R. J., *Evaluating Students by Classroom Observation: Watching Students Grow* (Washington, D.C.: National Education Association, 1984). A guide for use of performance assessment to evaluate student learning.

REFERENCE GUIDE

Annotated Bibliography on Applied Performance Testing. Center for Performance Assessment, Northwest Regional Educational Laboratory (101 S.W. Main Street, Suite 500, Portland, Oregon 97204). Contains numerous references on applied performance testing with information concerning the availability of each document.

7

Assembling, Administering, and Evaluating the Test

Assembling the test for use includes reviewing and editing the items . . . arranging the items in some logical order . . . and preparing clear directions. . . . After the test has been administered and scored, item analysis can help determine the effectiveness of each item. . . . Methods of item analysis differ for norm-referenced and criterion-referenced tests. . . . Item files contribute to testing effectiveness. . . . Computers can aid in test development and use.

When constructing items for an achievement test, it is usually desirable to prepare them at least a week or two in advance. A useful practice is to prepare a few items each day while instruction is under way and the material discussed in class is still fresh in mind. In any event, early preparation makes it possible to set the items aside for a time so that they can be reviewed later with a fresh outlook. It is also desirable to prepare more items than the test specifications call for, since defects are likely to become apparent in some items during the later review. The extra items will make it easier for you to maintain the distribution of items reflected in the set of specifications. If you are fortunate enough to end up with more good items than the specifications call for, you can store the extra items in an item file for future use.

Each test item prepared should be written on a separate card (such as a 5 × 8 index card). This simplifies the task of reviewing the items, arranging them in the test, and filing them for future use. The index card is also a convenient place for recording item-analysis data after the effectiveness of each item has been evaluated.

REVIEWING AND EDITING THE ITEMS

The pool of items for a particular test, after being set aside for a time, can be reviewed by the individual who constructed them or by a colleague. In either case it is helpful for the reviewer to read and answer each item as if taking the test. This provides a check on the correct answer and a means of spotting any obvious defects. A more careful evaluation of the items can be made by considering them in light of each of the following questions.

1. Does each test item measure an important learning outcome included in the test specifications?   Each test item should relate to one of the outcomes in the specifications, since each item is designed to measure one aspect of the subject matter and student performance specified there. If the outcome to which the item refers was noted on the card at the time the item was constructed, the task is simply to read the item and recheck its appropriateness. Essay questions and complex objective items may have to be checked against several outcomes in the specifications. In the final analysis each item should be related directly to the type of performance specified by the learning outcome(s) to be measured.

2. Is each item type appropriate for the particular learning outcome to be measured?   Some learning outcomes can be measured by any of the common item types. In such cases the multiple-choice item should be favored. However, if the learning outcome calls for supplying the answer, the completion or essay test must be used. If only two alternatives are plausible, the true-false item might be the most useful, and if the outcome calls for relating a series of homogeneous elements, the matching item might be more efficient. Reviewing the items provides for a second check on the appropriateness of each item type for the outcomes to be measured.

3. Does each item present a clearly formulated task?   The problem presented by a test item, regardless of item type, should be so clear and unambiguous that all students understand the task they are being called upon to perform. Those who fail an item should do so only because they lack the knowledge or intellectual skill called for by the item. Although ambiguity is a major problem in test construction, it is fortunately a flaw that becomes more apparent during a follow-up review of the items.

4. Is the item stated in simple, clear language?   This point is obviously related to the previous one, but here we are concerned more with the appropriateness of the reading level of the item for the age group to be tested. Except for technical terms that are a necessary part of the problem, the vocabulary should be simple. Similarly, short and simple sentences are to be favored over long and complex ones. Meeting these two standards is likely to help remove ambiguity but, equally important, they enable poor readers to demonstrate their levels of achievement more adequately. Reading ability is well worth measuring in its own right, but attempts should be made to keep it from interfering with the measurement of other learning outcomes. Ideally the reading level of the items should be adapted to the least able reader in the group to be tested.

5. Is the item free from extraneous clues? Although we do not want students to fail an item if they have achieved the outcome being measured, neither do we want them to answer an item correctly when they have *not* achieved the intended outcome. Thus, the review of items provides another opportunity to ferret out clues that might lead the uninformed to the correct answer. Verbal associations, grammatical inconsistencies, and other clues which are easily overlooked during the construction of the items frequently become obvious during review.

6. Is the difficulty of the item appropriate? As we noted earlier, the difficulty of the items in a criterion-referenced test should match the difficulty of the learning tasks set forth in the specific learning outcomes. No attempt should be made to alter item difficulty simply to obtain a spread of test scores. Since most criterion-referenced tests (for example, readiness pretests and formative tests) are used to measure student mastery, the items they contain typically have a relatively low level of difficulty. The important question here becomes, "Is the difficulty of the test item the same as that of the specified learning task?" We assume, of course, that the appropriateness of the learning task for the age group to be tested was checked at the time the list of learning outcomes was prepared.

In evaluating the difficulty of the items in a norm-referenced test, we shift our focus to the question. "How effectively will this item discriminate among students?" Recall that the purpose of a norm-referenced test is to obtain a dependable ranking of students, and that for us to do this we need items that discriminate. As we see later in this chapter in our discussion of item analysis, test items that are answered correctly by about half of the students provide for maximum discrimination between high and low achievers. Thus, items at that level of difficulty should be favored in our review of the items to be included in a norm-referenced test. Although easy items might be included early in the test for motivational purposes and difficult ones at the end to challenge the more able students, most of the items should fall near the 50 percent level of difficulty. In constructing norm-referenced tests, teachers typically err in constructing items that are too easy for the age group to be tested.

7. Is each test item independent, and are the items as a group free from overlapping? Knowing the answer to one item should not depend upon knowing the answer to another item. Thus, each item should be a separate scorable unit. Interlocking items are especially likely to occur when several items are based on common introductory material. A closely related problem occurs when information in one item helps the student determine the answer to another item. This is most common in tests that include both selection and supply items. Frequently the information given in selection items is useful in answering the supply items. These defects can easily be remedied by an overall review of the items during the final selection of the items to be included in the test.

8. Do the items to be included in the test provide adequate coverage of the test specifications?   The review, elimination, and revision of test items may result in a pool of items that deviates somewhat from the set of specifications. Thus, it may be necessary to further revise some of the items or to construct new ones. In any event the final selection of items for the test must be made in light of the test specifications in order to assure adequate sampling of the intended learning outcomes.

In addition to these general questions which apply to all item types, the rules for constructing each specific type of item provide criteria for item evaluation. In the review of multiple-choice items, for example, the completeness of the problem given in the stem, the inclusion of one clearly best answer, and the plausibility of the distracters all warrant special attention. Just before reviewing a pool of items, you should consult the Checklist for Evaluating Informal Achievement Tests presented in the Appendix.

ARRANGING THE ITEMS IN THE TEST

After the final selection of the items to be assembled into a test, a decision must be made concerning the best arrangement of the items. This arrangement will vary somewhat with the type of test being prepared. The following are useful guidelines for arranging items.

1. For instructional purposes it is usually desirable to group together items that measure the same learning outcome.   The instructional uses of test results tend to be enhanced when the items are arranged according to the learning outcomes measured. Typically all items measuring the same outcome are placed together and identified by an appropriate heading. The headings might be simply the major taxonomy categories ("Knowledge," "Comprehension," "Application," and so forth), statements of the general instructional objectives (for example, "Knows terms," "Knows basic principles"), or statements of the specific learning outcomes (for example, ""Defines terms," "Writes a sentence using each term"). Whether to group the items by general categories or by specific outcomes depends to a large extent on the type of test being prepared. For norm-referenced tests the general categories are usually sufficient. For criterion-referenced tests which are used typically to measure mastery and provide feedback concerning specific learning errors, arranging the items under each specific learning outcome is favored. The inclusion of the stated headings in the test helps the teacher to identify the types of learning outcomes causing difficulty and to plan group and individual remedial instruction.

2. Where possible, the items should be arranged so that all items of the same type are grouped together.   It is desirable to group together all multiple-choice items, all short-answer items, all true-false items, all essay questions, and so on. This arrangement makes it possible to provide only one set of directions for each item type. It also contributes to efficient test taking, since the student can maintain a uniform method of responding throughout each section. Finally, arranging by item type tends to simplify the scoring of the test and the analysis of the results.

If arrangement by item type conflicts with arrangement by learning outcome, grouping items by outcome should probably be favored because of the instructional value of doing so. Both types of arrangement can usually be accommodated, however, because achievement tests are typically limited to just a few item types, and because all items measuring a particular learning outcome tend to be of the same type.

3. The item should be arranged in order of increasing difficulty.   It is desirable to start with easy items and to establish an order of ascending difficulty throughout the test. Doing so will have a desirable motivational effect on students and will prevent the weaker students from "bogging down" on difficult items early in the test. If the items have been grouped by learning outcome, the outcomes can be arranged in order of increasing difficulty (for example, knowledge, comprehension, and application) and the items within each section can be arranged the same way. This system will closely approximate the desired order of increasing difficulty, while maintaining the basic arrangement by learning outcome.

It is obvious that only a limited number of different methods of arranging items can be applied to the same test. However, since most tests include only a few item types, it is usually possible to honor all three of the suggestions for item arrangement. If this is not feasible, the item arrangement that best fits the nature of the test and its intended use should be preferred. For most instructional purposes this means favoring arrangement by learning outcome.

PREPARING DIRECTIONS

The directions for an achievement test should be simple and concise and yet contain information concerning each of the following: (1) purpose of the test, (2) time allowed to complete the test, (3) how to record the answers, and (4) whether to guess when in doubt about the answer. The following sample directions for a multiple-choice test cover these four points.

EXAMPLE

Directions: This is a test of what you have learned during the first five weeks of the course. The results of this test will be used to clarify any points of difficulty and thus help you complete the course successfully.

There are 60 multiple-choice items, and you have one hour to complete the test.

For each item, select the answer that *best* completes the statement, or answers the question, and circle the letter of that answer.

Since your score will be the number of items answered correctly, *be sure to answer every item.*

When two or more item types are included in the same test, it is usually desirable to provide general directions for the test as a whole and specific directions for each part. When this is done, the general directions should contain the information about purpose, time allowed, and what to do about guessing, and the specific directions should describe how to record the answers for that particular part. Also, some items, such as keytype exercises, require special directions for each item.

The use of separate answer sheets requires some elaboration of the instructions for recording the answers. If students are not familiar with the use of separate answer sheets, it might also be desirable to present a sample item with the correct answer properly marked. There is a variety of separate answer sheets, and the specific instructions will have to be adapted to the particular type used. Unless machine scoring is to be used, however, a teacher-made answer sheet that simply lists the letters of the alternatives for each item is usually satisfactory:

ITEM	ANSWER
1.	A B C D E
2.	A B C D E
3.	A B C D E
4.	A B C D E

An answer sheet of this type should instruct the students to "put an X through the letter of the correct or best answer." Crossing out the answer is better than circling it, since an X is more visible than a circle through the holes in a scoring stencil. With this type of answer sheet, preparing a scoring key is simply a matter of punching out the letter of the correct answer for each item.

The Problem of Guessing

In our set of sample directions above, the students were told, "Since your score will be the number of items answered correctly, be sure to answer every item." This is an attempt to equalize the variation among students in their tendency to guess when in doubt about the answer. Such directions make it unnecessary for the instructor to correct for guessing. When students answer all items in a test, corrected and uncorrected scores rank students in exactly the same order. It is only when some items are omitted in a test that the correction makes a difference in student ranking.

There is considerable controversy concerning the issue of correcting test scores for guessing, but most of it is concerned with standardized testing. Since standardized achievement tests typically contain some material that is inappropriate for the group tested, and since all students may not have an opportunity to complete the test, directions warning them that there will be a penalty for guessing may be defensible. The aim here, of course, is to discourage students from attempting to improve their scores by guessing blindly at some of the answers. These directions do not have a uniform effect on students, however. The bold student is likely to continue to guess wildly, whereas the more hesitant student may even give up guessing on the basis of considerable knowledge.

Generally student scores on informal achievement tests should not be corrected for guessing. The material in the test is closely related to the learning experiences of the students, and the time limits are usually liberal enough to permit the students to carefully consider all items in the test. Under these conditions any guessing that is done is apt to be informed guessing. Although permitting such guessing may be objectionable under some conditions, guessing is quite similar to the behavior called for in making inferences, in identifying the probable causes and effects of an action, and in various decision-making aspects of problem solving. Thus, guessing is not entirely objectionable from an educational standpoint.

There may be some courses or some units within a course in which preciseness receives so much emphasis during instruction that it is desirable to stress it also during testing. In this case, "do-not-guess" instructions would be appropriate. They would also be appropriate in a speed test—that is, a test in which the students have insufficient time to consider all the items. In both instances the students should be told that there will be a correction for guessing, and the following correction-for-guessing formula should be applied during the scoring.

$$\text{Score} \; = \; \text{Right} \; - \; \frac{\text{Wrong}}{n \, - \, 1}$$

In this formula, n equals the number of alternatives in each item. Thus, for a multiple-choice test whose items contained four alternatives, the formula would be as follows:

$$\text{Score} \; = \; \text{Right} \; - \; \frac{\text{Wrong}}{3}$$

Applying this correction-for-guessing formula involves simply counting the number of right answers and the number of wrong answers on a student's test paper and inserting these numbers in the formula. The omitted items are not counted. Thus, a student who answered 40 items correctly and 6 items incorrectly on a 50-item multiple-choice test using four alternatives would receive a corrected score that is computed as follows:

$$40 \; - \; \frac{6}{3} \; = \; 40 \; - \; 2 \; = \; 38$$

The assumption here is that the student guessed on 8 items and had chance success (that is, 2 right, 6 wrong). The formula simply removes those 2 right answers that can be accounted for by chance success in guessing.

REPRODUCING THE TEST

When the test is typed for reproduction, the items should be spaced on the page so that they are easy for students to read and easy for the instructor to score. If multiple-choice items are used, the alternatives should be listed underneath the stem, as in the examples presented in Chapter 3. All of the parts of an item should be on the same page. For interpretive exercises, however, it may be necessary to place the introductory material on a facing page or on a separate sheet to be handed out with the test.

If the answers are to be marked on the test itself, provision should be made for recording the answers on the left side of the page. This simplifies the scoring. If separate answer sheets are to be used and the test is to be administered to more than one group of students, it is usually necessary to warn the students not to make any marks on the test booklets. It is also wise to make more copies of the test than are needed because some students will ignore your warning.

Achievement tests for classroom use are commonly reproduced by the mimeograph, ditto, photocopy, or photo-offset processes. Although mimeographing is satisfactory for most purposes, the use of drawings or pictures requires one of the other methods. Regardless of the method of reproduction used, the master copy should be checked carefully for item arrangement, legibility, accuracy of detail in drawings, and freedom from typographical errors.

ADMINISTERING AND SCORING THE TEST

The administration of a carefully prepared informal achievement test is largely a matter of providing proper working conditions, keeping interruptions to a minimum, and arranging enough space between students to prevent cheating. The written directions should be clear enough to make the test self-administering, but in some situations it may be desirable to give the directions orally as well. With young students a blackboard illustration may also be useful. Above all, make certain that all the students know exactly what to do, and then provide them with the most favorable conditions in which to do it.

Scoring is facilitated if all answers are recorded on the left side of each test page, as we suggested earlier. Under this arrangement, scoring is simply a matter of marking the correct answers on a copy of the test and placing it next to the column of answers on each student's paper. If a separate answer sheet is used, it is usually better to punch out the letters of the correct answers on a copy of the answer sheet and use this as a scoring stencil. The stencil is laid over each answer sheet and the correctly marked answers appear through the holes. Where no mark appears, a red line can be drawn across the hole. This indicates to the student the correct answer for each item missed. If machine scoring is to be used, simply scan the students' papers to make certain that only one answer was marked for each item.

Unless corrected for guessing, a student's score on an objective test is typically the number of answers marked correctly. Thus, each test item is counted as one point. Although teachers frequently desire to count some items more heavily than others because of their importance or difficulty, such weighting of scores complicates the scoring task and seldom results in an improved measure of achievement. A better way to increase the relative weight of an area is to construct more items in that area.

ITEM ANALYSIS OF NORM-REFERENCED TESTS

After a test has been administered and scored, it is usually desirable to evaluate the effectiveness of the items. This is done by studying the students' responses to each item. When formalized, the procedure is called *item analysis,* and it provides information concerning how well each item in the test functioned. Since the item-analysis procedures for norm-referenced and criterion-referenced tests differ, they will be considered separately. In this section we will discuss norm-referenced tests (that is, tests designed to discriminate among students).

The item-analysis procedure for norm-referenced tests provides the following information:

1. The difficulty of the item.
2. The discriminating power of the item.
3. The effectiveness of each alternative.

Thus, item-analysis information can tell us if a norm-referenced item was too easy or too hard, how well it discriminated between high and low scorers on the test, and whether all of the alternatives functioned as intended. Item-analysis data also help us detect specific technical flaws, and thus provide further information for improving test items.

Even if we have no intention of reusing the items, item analysis has several benefits. First, it provides useful information for class discussion of the test. For example, easy items can be skipped over or treated lightly, answers to difficult items can be explained more fully, and defective items can be pointed out to students rather than defended as fair. Second, item analysis provides data that help students improve their learning. The frequency with which each incorrect answer is chosen reveals common errors and misconceptions, which provide a focus for remedial work. Third, item analysis provides insights and skills that lead to the preparation of better tests in the future. The process helps us become more aware of defective items and how to correct them.

A Simplified Item-Analysis
Procedure for Norm-Referenced Tests

There are a number of different item-analysis procedures that might be applied to norm-referenced tests. For informal achievement tests used in teaching, only the simplest of procedures seems warranted. The following steps outline a simple but effective procedure. We shall use 32 test papers to illustrate the steps.

1. Arrange all 32 test papers in order from the highest score to the lowest score.

2. Select approximately one third of the papers with the highest scores and call this the *upper* group (10 papers). Select the same number of papers with the lowest scores and call this the *lower* group (10 papers). Set the middle group of papers aside (12 papers). Although these could be included in the analysis, using only the upper and lower groups simplifies the procedure.

3. For each item, count the number of students in the *upper* group who selected each alternative. Make the same count for the *lower* group.

4. Record the count from step 3 on a copy of the test, in columns to the left of the alternatives to which each count refers. The count may also be recorded on the item card or on a separate sheet, as follows:

ITEM 1. ALTERNATIVES	A	B*	C	D	E
Upper 10	0	6	3	1	0
Lower 10	3	2	2	3	0

* = correct answer

5. Estimate *item difficulty* by determining the percentage of students who answered the item correctly. The simplest procedure is to base this estimate only on those students included in the item-analysis groups. Thus, sum the number of students in the upper and lower groups (10 + 10 = 20); sum the number of students who selected the correct answer (for item 1, above, 6 + 2 = 8); and divide the first sum into the second and multiply by 100, as follows:

$$\text{Index of Item Difficulty} = \frac{8}{20} \times 100 = 40\%$$

Although our computation is based on the upper and lower groups only, it provides a close approximation of the estimate that would be obtained with the total group. Thus, it is proper to say that the index of difficulty for this item is 40 percent (for this particular group). Note that since "difficulty" refers to the *percentage answering the item correctly*, the smaller the percentage figure the more difficult the item.

The formula for computing item difficulty is as follows:

$$P = \frac{R}{T} \times 100$$

where P = the percentage who answered the item correctly; R = the number who answered the item correctly; and T = the total number who tried the item.

6. Estimate *item discriminating power* by comparing the number of students in the upper and lower groups who answered the item correctly. Note in our sample item that 6 students in the upper group and 2 students in the lower group selected the

correct answer. This indicates *positive discrimination,* since the item differentiates between students in the same way that the total test score does. That is, students with high scores on the test (the upper group) answered the item correctly more frequently than students with low scores on the test (the lower group).

Although analysis by inspection may be all that is necessary for most purposes, an index of discrimination can easily be computed. Simply subtract the number in the lower group who answered the item correctly from the number in the upper group who answered the item correctly, and divide by the number in *each* group. For our sample item the computation would be as follows:

$$\text{Index of Item Discriminating Power} = \frac{6 - 2}{10} = .40$$

Thus, the formula for computing item discriminating power is as follows:

$$D = \frac{Ru - R_L}{\frac{1}{2} T}$$

where D = the index of discriminating power; Ru = the number in the upper group who answered the item correctly; R_L = the number in the lower group who answered the item correctly; and $\frac{1}{2} T$ = one half of the total number of students included in the item analysis.

The discriminating power of an item is reported as a decimal fraction; maximum positive discriminating power is indicated by an index of 1.00. This is obtained *only* when all students in the upper group answer correctly and no one in the lower group does. For our illustrative upper and lower groups of 10, the computation for an item with maximum discriminating power would be as follows:

$$D = \frac{10 - 0}{10} = 1.00$$

Note that this item is at the 50 percent level of difficulty (the upper 10 answered it correctly; and the lower 10 missed it). This explains why test makers are encouraged to prepare items at the 50 percent level of difficulty for norm-referenced tests. *It is only at this level that maximum discrimination is possible.*

Zero discriminating power (.00) is obtained when an equal number of students in each group answers the item correctly. Negative discriminating power is obtained when more students in the lower group than in the upper group answer correctly. Both types of items should be removed from norm-referenced tests and then discarded or improved.

7. Determine the *effectiveness of the distracters* by comparing the number of students in the upper and lower groups who selected each incorrect alternative. A good distracter will attract more students from the lower group than the upper group. Thus, in step 4 of our illustrative item analysis it can be seen that alternatives

A and D are functioning effectively, alternative C is poor since it attracted more students from the upper group, and alternative E is completely ineffective since it attracted no one. An analysis such as this is useful in evaluating a test item and when combined with an inspection of the item itself, it provides helpful information for improving the item.

These suggested steps for analyzing items can be modified to fit particular situations. In some cases inspecting the data, rather than computing the difficulty and discriminating power, may be all that is necessary. Also, in selecting the upper and lower groups it may be desirable to use the top and bottom 25 percent if the group is large, or the upper and lower halves if the group is small. The important thing is to use a large enough fraction of the group to provide useful information. Selecting the top and bottom 27 percent of the group (as is recommended for more refined analysis) and applying other statistical refinements is seldom warranted with classroom achievement tests.

Interpreting Item-Analysis Data on Norm-Referenced Tests

Since a relatively small number of students is used when classroom tests are analyzed, item-analysis information should be interpreted with great caution. Both the difficulty and the discriminating power of an item can be expected to vary from one group to another. Thus, it does not seem wise to set a minimum level of discriminating power for the selection of items, or to distinguish between items on the basis of small differences in their indexes of discrimination. Other things being equal, we should favor items at the 50 percent level of difficulty and items with the highest discriminating power. However, the tentative nature of our data requires that we allow for a wide margin of error. If an item provides a positive index of discrimination, if all of the alternatives are functioning effectively, and if the item measures an educationally significant outcome, it should be retained and placed in an item file for future use.

When items are kept in an item file and reused after a period of time, it is a good practice to record the item-analysis data on the card each time the item is used. An accumulation of such data will show the variability in an item's indexes of difficulty and discriminating power and thus make the information more interpretable.

ITEM ANALYSIS OF CRITERION-REFERENCED TESTS

Since criterion-referenced tests are designed to describe which learning tasks a student can and cannot perform rather than to discriminate among students, the traditional indexes of item difficulty and item discriminating power are of little value. A set of items in a criterion-referenced mastery test, for example, might be answered correctly by all students (zero discriminating power) and still be effective items. If the items closely match an important learning outcome, the results simply tell us that here is an outcome that all students have mastered. This is valuable information for describing the types of tasks students can perform, and to eliminate such items from the test would distort our description of student learning.

The difficulty of an item in a criterion-referenced test is determined by the learning task it is designed to measure. If the task is easy, the item should be easy. If the task is difficult, the item should be difficult. No attempt should be made to eliminate easy items or to alter item difficulty simply to obtain a spread of test scores. Although an index of item difficulty can be computed for items in a criterion-referenced test, there is seldom a need to do so. If mastery is being measured and the instruction has been effective, criterion-referenced test items are typically answered correctly by a large percentage of the students.

Item-Analysis Procedure for Criterion-Referenced Tests

A basic concern in evaluating the items in a criterion-referenced mastery test is the extent to which each item is measuring the *effects of instruction*. If an item can be answered correctly by all students both *before* and *after* instruction, the item obviously is not measuring instructional effects. Similarly, if an item is answered incorrectly by all students both before and after instruction, the item is not serving its intended function. These are extreme examples, of course, but they highlight the importance of obtaining a measure of instructional effects as one basis for determining item quality.

To obtain a measure of item effectiveness based on instructional effects, the teacher must give the same test before instruction and after instruction. Effective items will be answered correctly by a larger number of students after instruction than before instruction. An index of *sensitivity to instructional effect(s)*[1] can be computed by using the following formula:

$$S = \frac{R_A - R_B}{T}$$

where R_A the number of students answering the item correctly *after* instruction; R_B = the number answering correctly *before* instruction; and T the total number answering the item both times. Applying this formula to an item that was answered incorrectly by all students before instruction and correctly by all students after instruction ($N = 32$), our result would be as follows:

$$S = \frac{32 - 0}{32} = 1.00$$

Thus, maximum sensitivity to instructional effects is indicated by an index of 1.00. The index for effective items will fall between .00 and 1.00, with larger positive values indicating items with greater sensitivity to the effects of instruction.

[1]W. J. Kryspin and J. T. Feldhusen, *Developing Classroom Tests* (Minneapolis: Burgess Publishing Co., 1974) p. 166.

There are several limitations in the use of the sensitivity index. (1) The test must be given twice to compute the index. (2) A low index may be due to either an ineffective item or ineffective instruction. (3) The item responses after instruction may be influenced to some extent by having taken the same test earlier. The last limitation is likely to be most serious where the instruction time is short. Despite these limitations, the sensitivity index provides a useful means of evaluating the effectiveness of items in a criterion-referenced mastery test. Items are of little value for measuring the intended outcomes of instruction unless they are sensitive to instructional effects.

A number of other statistical procedures have been proposed for analyzing criterion-referenced test items. For a review and critique of the methods see Berk (1984).

USING A TEST-ITEM FILE

After test items have been used and evaluated, it is desirable to make any corrections needed (e.g., change wording, replace poor distracters) and then to place the items in a test file. If each item has been placed on a 5 × 8 index card, as suggested earlier, item-analysis data can be placed on the back of the card and the cards can be filed by content area and objective measured. The sample card in Figure 7.1, for example, would be filed under the first subcategory of the general content heading "Test Planning," as follows:

TEST PLANNING

Knowledge
Understanding
Application

If a more detailed filing system is desired, Test Planning can be subdivided into such categories as Instructional Objectives, Test Specifications, and the like. Similarly, the general categories for objectives can also be further subdivided (e.g., Knowledge of Terms, Knowledge of Facts, Knowledge of Principles). The amount of detail in the filing system depends on how extensive the file is to become and how the items are to be used. A test file for a mastery learning program, for example, will need to be very detailed so that test items for brief learning units can be easily selected.

The test-item file is valuable in its own right and is assuming increasing importance as computers become more widely used in school testing. Item files maintained by teachers provide good beginning pools of items for starting computer item banks needed in computer-assisted test construction.

COMPUTER USE IN TESTING

The wide use of computers in the schools has enabled teachers to turn over many of the procedures of test development and use to the computer. A complete system can

Course *Test Construction*   Unit *Test Planning*
Objective *Identifies the meaning of terms (Knowledge)*

ITEM

The term *taxonomy* means
  *A. classification
   B. identification
   C. interpretation
   D. specification

(Front of item card)

ITEM DATA

| Date | Students | ALTERNATIVES | | | | | INDEXES | |
		A	B	C	D	Total	Diff.	Disc.
1/5/86	Upper	10	0	0	0	10	80%	.40
	Lower	6	1	1	2	10		
4/25/87	Upper	9	0	0	1	10	65%	.50
	Lower	4	3	0	3	10		
	Upper							
	Lower							
	Upper							
	Lower							

(Back of item card)

FIGURE 7.1. Test Item Card with Item-Analysis Data Recorded on Back.

provide for item banking, test printing, test scoring, statistical analysis, and the maintenance of student records. Some test publishers provide complete management systems that incorporate all of these elements in programs for individualized instruction. Computerized "adaptive" or "tailored" testing is also being developed and in the future may make paper-and-pencil testing obsolete.

Item Banking

Computers are especially useful for maintaining files of items (called item banks, item pools) that can be retrieved later for the preparation of tests. Typically the items are coded by subject area, instructional level, instructional objective measured, and various pertinent item characteristics (e.g., item difficulty and discriminating power). The coded information for each item makes it possible to retrieve items with known characteristics and thus build tests that match given test specifications. The flexibility and efficiency of the computer should contribute to the more effective uses of item banks and relieve the test user of many of the routine tasks involved in maintaining an item file.

Test Printing

The custom designed tests based on the items selected from the computer item bank can also be printed by the computer. The coded information recorded for each item makes it possible to arrange the test in the form desired. For example, the computer might be directed to arrange the items by instructional objective with the set of items under each objective in order of increasing difficulty.

Test Scoring and Statistical Analysis

After the test is administered, the computer can be used to score the test, analyze and arrange the scores in various ways, compute item-analysis data for each item, and provide reliability information. The specific nature of the data provided depends on the computer program that is used. The role of the computer in scoring and statistical analysis is especially helpful in relieving test users of tasks that can be very time consuming. Thus, it is likely to encourage test users to analyze and use the test results in ways that otherwise tend to be neglected.

Maintenance of Student Records

Records of student performance can be maintained in the computer in various forms so that learning progress can be readily determined. In a mastery learning program, for example, a student's record might indicate what objectives have been mastered, what areas show lack of mastery, and what types of learning errors are occurring in the nonmastered areas. The detailed information that can be stored in the computer and easily retrieved when needed should contribute to greater instructional use of achievement tests.

Computerized Adaptive Testing

In addition to the various ways that the computer can assist in paper-and-pencil testing, it can also be used directly in "adaptive" or "tailored" testing. This involves the computer administration of a set of test items that is most appropriate for each individual's achievement or ability level. The examinee is presented with test items on the computer screen and the answer to each item (or to all previous items) determines which item will be administered next by the computer. Thus, each person is tested with an individually tailored test drawn from the same pool of items. Adapting the test to each examinee's performance level eliminates those items that are too easy and too difficult for the individual. This makes it possible to obtain a more effective measure of achievement with fewer test items than is possible with the typical paper-and-pencil test.

In addition to the psychometric efficiency of computer adaptive testing, it provides for more controlled conditions of test administration and for the immediate availability of results. All examinees are tested under the same standard conditions and the computer can score and report the results without the usual delays involved in the scoring, transfer, and analysis of test data. This immediate reporting saves time and avoids the errors that commonly occur in the scoring and transfer of scores. The immediate availability of results should also contribute to the greater instructional use of test scores.

As computers become more widely used in the classroom, we can expect computer-assisted testing and computer adaptive testing to play an increasingly important role. This will relieve teachers of many of the time-consuming, routine tasks presently connected with testing and, hopefully, will bring about a better integration of testing and teaching.

CHECKLIST FOR EVALUATING INFORMAL ACHIEVEMENT TESTS

In order to simplify the task of reviewing and evaluating newly constructed achievement tests, a checklist has been placed in the Appendix. This checklist includes a comprehensive list of points that are in harmony with sound test construction principles. Since the items in the checklist are based on the first seven chapters of this book, it provides a review of points to consider during test construction, as well as a useful guide for evaluating the final draft of a test.

SUMMARY OF POINTS

The emphasis in this chapter can be summarized by the following points.

1. Test items should be recorded on index cards and set aside for a time before reviewing them.
2. A review of each test item should focus on the importance, relevance, and difficulty of the task presented and the clarity with which it is stated.
3. Where needed, items should be edited to remove nonfunctioning material, barriers that might prevent a knowledgeable person from responding (e.g., ambiguity), and clues that might lead the uninformed to the correct answer (e.g., verbal associations).
4. The items selected for a test should be guided by test specifications to assure adequate coverage of the outcomes to be measured.
5. Item arrangement within the test will vary with the type of test used, but where possible, items should be grouped by the major outcome measured (e.g., knowledge, comprehension, application). Similar item types should be grouped together, and the items should be arranged in order of increasing difficulty within sections.

6. Test directions should indicate the purpose of the test, the time allowed, how to record the answers, and whether to guess when in doubt.

7. On most classroom tests, students should be told to answer every question. The correction for guessing should be limited to speed tests and to those few areas where guessing is contrary to the learning outcomes being measured.

8. When the test copy is being reproduced it should be checked for proper item arrangement, spacing, legibility, accuracy of detail in drawings, and freedom from typographical errors.

9. Test administration should provide conditions that permit all students to demonstrate their best performance (e.g., good work space, no interruptions) without the aid of others (e.g., sufficient space between seats).

10. Scoring is typically based on one point for each objective test item.

11. Item analysis of norm-referenced tests provides an index of item difficulty and item discriminating power for each item and provides for an evaluation of the effectiveness of each distracter.

12. One item-analysis procedure used with criterion-referenced tests provides an index of sensitivity to instructional effects. This index is based on a comparison of test responses before and after instruction.

13. Item analysis of classroom tests must be interpreted with caution because of the small number of students that is typically used.

14. A test-item file is useful for building up a pool of items for future use. A simple procedure involves writing each item on an index card and recording item-analysis data on the back each time it is used.

15. Computers can be used for item banking, test printing, test scoring, statistical analysis, maintenance of student records, and the direct administration of tests "adapted" or "tailored" to each individual's ability or achievement level.

16. The use of computers should contribute to the more effective use of tests in teaching.

ADDITIONAL READING

BERK, R. A., ED., *A Guide to Criterion-Referenced Test Construction* (Baltimore, Maryland: Johns Hopkins University Press, 1984). See Chapter 5 by R. A. Berk, "Conducting the Item Analysis," for a review and critique of various methods for analyzing criterion-referenced test items. See Chapter 4 by Jason Millman, "Individualizing Test Construction and Administration by Computer," for a description of item banking and adaptive testing.

CUNNINGHAM, G. K., *Educational and Psychological Measurement* (New York: Macmillan Publishing Co., Inc., 1986). See Chapter 4, "Computer Applications to Measurement," for descriptions of computer use in item analysis, item banking, tailor-made testing, scoring, and statistical analyses.

GRONLUND, N. E., *Measurement and Evaluation in Teaching*, 5th ed. (New York: Macmillan Publishing Co., Inc., 1985), Chapter 10. Describes how to assemble, administer, and appraise tests, including norm-referenced and criterion-referenced item analysis.

MEHRENS, W. A., AND I. J. LEHMANN, *Measurement and Evaluation in Education and Psychology*, 3rd ed. (New York: Holt, Rinehart and Winston, Inc., 1984). See Chapter 8, "Assembling, Reproducing, Administering, Scoring and Analyzing Classroom Achievement Tests" for another discussion of the topics covered in this chapter.

8

Interpreting Test Results

Test results can be interpreted in two basic ways. . . . Criterion-referenced interpretation describes the types of performance a student can demonstrate. . . . Norm-referenced interpretation describes how a student's performance compares to that of others. . . . Both types of interpretation are sensible . . . and each provides unique information concerning student achievement. . . . Various statistics can be used to describe a set of test scores.

After a measure of achievement has been obtained, the results need to be put in a form that is readily interpretable. How the results are organized and presented depends to a large extent on the type of interpretation to be made. If we are to use the results to describe the nature of a student's performance on a particular set of learning tasks (criterion-referenced interpretation), our analysis and presentation may need to be considerably detailed. On the other hand, if we simply wish to indicate a student's level of performance in comparison to others (norm-referenced interpretation), some method of indicating relative standing in an appropriate reference group is all that is needed. In certain instances we may, of course, wish to use both types of interpretation for the same test.

Combining the two types of interpretation is most likely to be effective where norm-referenced interpretation is added to the performance description of a criterion-referenced test. For example, we might say that a student "can correctly spell all of the words" on some clearly defined word list and that "only 10 percent of sixth graders can do this." Many users of criterion-referenced tests demand these additional comparative interpretations so that they can determine "how good" the described performance is for the student's particular stage of learning.

When criterion-referenced interpretations are added to tests designed for norm-referenced interpretation, our descriptions of student performance are likely to suffer. Since norm-referenced tests typically cover a broad range of learning outcomes with a few items per outcome, the performance descriptions tend to be sketchy and unreliable. In addition, the easy items are typically removed from norm-referenced tests to increase the test's discriminating power and, thus, the descriptions of the tasks that students can perform will be incomplete. This is a serious problem in describing the performance of low achievers because many of the tasks they are able to perform have been removed from the test.

In this chapter our discussion will be restricted to those elementary methods of interpreting test results that are commonly used with informal achievement tests, and we assume that the test was specifically constructed to maximize the method of interpretation being used. A summary of the methods of interpretation to be described in this chapter is presented in Figure 8.1.

It will be noted in Figure 8.1 that a criterion-referenced interpretation can be limited to a simple description of the tasks that a student can perform, or it can involve a comparison of the student's performance to some performance standard. In either case, it does not require comparing the student's performance to the performance of others.

Norm-referenced interpretation involves some means of showing how an individual's test score compares to the scores of others in some known group. Although there are many different methods of expressing such test scores, our discussion is limited to the methods shown in Figure 8.1. For descriptions of other types of norm-referenced scores see Gronlund (1985) and Lyman (1986).

FIGURE 8.1.   Common Criterion-Referenced Methods and Norm-Referenced Methods for Interpreting Informal Achievement Test Results.

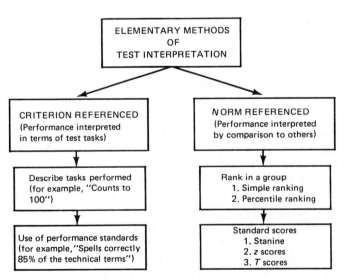

In addition to describing the elementary methods of test interpretation shown in Figure 8.1, a few statistics for describing a set of test scores are also presented.

CRITERION-REFERENCED INTERPRETATION

In both the construction and the interpretation of a criterion-referenced test,[1] the focus is on obtaining as clear a description of an individual's test performance as possible. If the test has been constructed to measure a clearly defined achievement domain, the domain specifications provide the framework for test interpretation. More commonly, however, criterion-referenced test results are interpreted in terms of instructional objectives, or some other meaningful cluster of test items. This is partly due to the varying conceptions of criterion-referenced testing among educational practitioners and partly due to the present state of criterion-referenced measurement technology (Berk, 1984). Methods of clearly defining achievement domains is an emerging art that currently is most easily applied and illustrated in the basic skill areas. It is hoped that further developments in technology will result in more sophisticated descriptive schemes that can be effectively applied in all areas of study.

Performance Descriptions

Because criterion-referenced testing is commonly used to measure mastery or minimum competency, it is frequently assumed that a standard or cut-off score is required for interpretation. There is nothing in the nature of criterion-referenced testing, however, that demands a cut-off score. The *criterion* referred to in the term *criterion-referenced test* is not the cut-off score, as assumed by some, but the domain of tasks being measured. Thus, criterion-referenced test results can be used to simply describe an individual's performance on a set of tasks. For example, we might make descriptive statements like the following:

Distinguishes between properly and improperly stated instructional objectives.
States instructional objectives as learning outcomes.
Identifies technical flaws in test items.
Constructs test items that are free of technical defects.

Although general descriptive statements such as these may be useful for some evaluation purposes and for general reporting, a more detailed analysis of test results is desirable for instructional purposes. An item-by-item analysis like that shown in Table 8.1 is especially useful in identifying student learning errors. By looking across the rows in the table, one can evaluate the performance of each

[1]The terms *domain-referenced* and *objective-referenced* have also been used to describe tests that are interpreted as described here. The term *criterion-referenced* test has been so widely used in the literature, however, that it is preferred.

TABLE 8.1   Portion of an Item-Response Chart Showing Correct ($+$) and Incorrect ($-$) Responses to Items on a Criterion-Referenced Test

OBJECTIVES	→ KNOWS BASIC TERMS											
CONTENT AREAS	→ TAXONOMY			TEST PLANNING			ITEM WRITING			ITEM ANALYSIS		
Item nos.	→ 1	2	3	4	5	6	7	8	9	10	11	12
Jim Astor	+	+	+	+	+	+	+	+	−	+	+	−
Edna Bright	+	+	+	+	+	+	+	−	−	+	−	−
Dick Charles	+	+	−	+	+	+	−	−	+	−	+	−
Tricia Deere	+	+	+	+	+	+	+	+	+	−	+	−
Derek Edward	+	+	+	+	−	−	−	−	−	+	−	−
Erik Todd	+	+	−	−	−	−	+	−	−	−	−	−

student and pinpoint the specific errors. By looking down the columns in the table, one can determine the pattern of class responses for each item and each cluster of items. Table 8.1 contains only a portion of an item-response chart. The complete chart would include more objectives, more items, and a larger number of students. Here we are simply illustrating a useful format for interpreting criterion-referenced test results.

An item-response chart is especially useful in formative testing (that is, testing to improve learning) since the detailed analysis provides the type of information needed for making specific feedback-corrective prescriptions for each student. A common procedure is to have a prespecified set of corrective procedures (e.g., pages to read, programmed materials, or visual aids) keyed to each test item or each objective. Assigning remedial work to an individual student is then simply a matter of checking the corrective prescriptions that match the items answered incorrectly.

The item-response chart is also useful in checking on both the test and the instruction. Where a large number of students answer an item incorrectly, it is possible that either the item is defective or that the instruction was faulty. Item 12 in Table 8.1, for example, should be checked carefully to determine why all students answered it incorrectly. If the item is of good quality, then the instruction most likely needs to be modified.

Use of Performance Standards

When criterion-referenced tests are used to distinguish between those who have mastered a given set of tasks and those who have not, some standard or cut-off score must be set. This standard might be in terms of the speed of performance (e.g., "solves ten computational problems in two minutes"), the precision of the performance (for example, "measures an obtuse angle to the nearest whole degree"), or the percentage of items answered correctly (e.g., "defines 85 percent of the basic terms"). The percentage-correct score is widely used in judging whether objectives have been mastered and thus in reporting the results on criterion-referenced mastery tests.

A simplified individual report form using a percentage-correct standard is presented in Figure 8.2. Here the standard for mastery was set at 85, and the report shows that this student has mastered all objectives except one. Although the setting of performance standards is somewhat arbitrary, it provides a useful basis for planning remedial work. If a majority of students has failed to master an objective, remedial instruction can be planned for the entire group. If a small number of students has fallen short of mastery, individual remedial work can be prescribed. An item-by-item response chart, like the one described earlier, can also be made for the unmastered objectives to pinpoint the student's learning errors.

Setting Performance Standards. Setting standards of acceptable performance on a criterion-referenced mastery test is both difficult and frustrating because there are so many issues involved and so few clear guidelines to follow. We must depend largely on judgments based on our own teaching experience and, if a committee is involved, on the experiences of our fellow teachers. A relatively simple and practical procedure is to arbitrarily set a standard and then adjust it up or down as various conditions and experiences are considered. For example, we might use an approach like the following in setting a performance standard for a particular domain of tasks.

1. Set mastery level on a multiple-choice test at 85 percent correct.
2. Increase the level if essential for next stage of instruction.
3. Increase the level if essential for safety (e.g., mixing chemicals).
4. Increase the level if test or subtest is short.
5. Decrease the level if repetition is provided at next stage.
6. Decrease the level if tasks have low relevance.

FIGURE 8.2. Individual Report Form for a Criterion-Referenced Mastery Test.

TEST	Educational Measurement		STUDENT	Bob Jones
MASTERY	85% correct			

OBJECTIVE	NUMBER CORRECT	PERCENTAGE CORRECT	MASTERED (X)
1. Knows terms (20)*	18	90	X
2. Knows procedures (20)	18	90	X
3. Comprehends principles (20)	17	85	X
4. Applies principles (20)	14	60	
5. Interprets data (20)	17	85	X

*Number of items for each objective.

7. Decrease the level if tasks are extremely difficult.
8. Adjust the level up or down as teaching experience dictates.

In using this procedure, one should adjust the starting percentage-correct score for the types of test items to be used. For short-answer items a lower scale should be used (say 80 percent correct), while a higher score should be used for true-false items (say 95 percent correct). This is to allow for differences in chances of guessing the correct answers. It would also be desirable to add other adjustment factors, as they become evident from experience, to the list for future use.

Although the procedure we have described for setting performance standards is a crude one, it is better than arbitrarily setting the standard at 85 percent correct and not adjusting it to meet special considerations. For descriptions of more complex methods of setting standards and discussions of the problems and issues surrounding standards setting, see Berk (1984).

NORM-REFERENCED INTERPRETATION

Since norm-referenced tests are designed to indicate how an individual's test performance compares to that of others, test interpretation is concerned with determining each individual's relative standing in a reference group. For the classroom teacher this typically means comparing the student to the classroom group. For comparison purposes, it is common to use the total raw score on the test or a score that has been derived from the raw score. Our discussion here will be confined to a few simplified methods of treating raw scores and to the computation of *percentile ranks* and *stanines*. Both are easily computed and can be used with classroom tests. Other standard scores will be described later in the chapter.

Simple Ranking of Raw Scores

A commn method of presenting the scores on a norm-referenced test to a classroom group is to simply list the scores on the blackboard. This is typically done by arranging the scores in rank order from high to low and making a frequency count to show the number (N) of students earning each score. A sample frequency distribution of this type is presented in columns 1 and 2 in Table 8.2 (ignore columns 3 and 4 for now). By looking at the simple ranking of raw scores for these 30 students ($N = 30$), each student could easily determine his or her relative standing in the group.

Percentile Ranks

Although a simple ranking of raw scores is useful in providing feedback to students on a norm-referenced test, it has a major limitation when it is used to communicate test results to others. Ranking tenth is fairly high in a group of thirty but not in a group of ten. To overcome this difficulty caused by variations in group size, scores are frequently converted to percentile ranks. A percentile rank indicates a student's relative position in a group in terms of the percentage of group members scoring at or below the student's score. For example, if a raw score of 33 equals a

TABLE 8.2 Frequency Distribution and Percentile Ranks for an Objective Test of 40 Items

1 TEST SCORE	2 FREQUENCY	3 CUMULATIVE FREQUENCY	4 PERCENTILE* RANK
38	1	30	98
37	1	29	95
36	0	28	93
35	2	28	90
34	1	26	85
33	2	25	80
32	3	23	72
31	2	20	63
30	1	18	58
29	4	17	50
28	2	13	40
27	2	11	33
26	2	9	27
25	3	7	18
24	1	4	12
23	0	3	10
22	1	3	8
21	1	2	5
20	0	1	3
19	1	1	2
	$N = 30$		

*Rounded to nearest whole number.

percentile rank of 80, it means 80 percent of the group members had raw scores equal to or lower than 33. By converting to percentile ranks, we put our raw scores on a scale that has the same meaning with different sized groups and that is readily understood by test users.

A simple formula for converting raw scores to percentile ranks is the following (where *PR* stands for percentile rank):

$$PR = \frac{\text{number of students below score} + \frac{1}{2} \text{ of students at score}}{\text{number in group } (N)} \times 100$$

This formula was used to compute the percentile ranks in Table 8.2. The steps include (1) adding the score frequencies from the bottom up (that is, adding each score's frequency to the total frequency of all lower scores) to obtain the cumulative frequency (column 3), and (2) applying the formula at each score level to get the percentile rank (column 4). For example, the raw score 30 has 17 scores below it and one score at that score level. Thus, the percentile rank for raw score 30 would be computed as follows:

$$PR = \frac{17 + .5}{30} \times 100 = 58.3$$

Percentile ranks are rounded to the nearest whole number, so Table 8.2 shows a percentile rank of 58 for raw score 30. You can obtain practice with this procedure by computing the percentile ranks for other score levels in Table 8.2 and checking your answers with those in the table.

When using percentile ranks there are two cautions to be kept in mind: (1) Percentile ranks refer to the *percentage of persons* earning lower scores and *not* to the percentage of items answered correctly. (2) Percentile ranks are always specific to the particular group for which they are computed. For example, a percentile rank of 90 in a gifted group represents considerably higher performance than a percentile rank of 90 in an average group. Thus, whenever we are describing a student's relative performance, knowing the nature of the group is just as important as knowing the student's relative standing.

Using the Stanine System of Standard Scores

In teaching we frequently like to compare a student's relative achievement on different tests, or compare the student's standing on a test with the standing of that individual on some other measure of achievement (for instance, an assessment of theme writing or a rating of laboratory performance). Similarly, in assigning and reporting grades, we need some means of combining such diverse elements as test scores, ratings, and evaluations of various types of written work into a composite score or final grade. This task is usually complicated by our desire to weight some elements more than others. These and similar problems require that we make all the data comparable by converting them to a common scale.

A number of different systems of standard scores are useful for comparing or combining test scores and other types of data. The system that is simplest to understand and use is the *stanine* (pronounced staynine) system. This system is not only useful for classroom achievement tests but is also used widely with standardized tests of all types. This is an additional advantage, in that students' scores on classroom tests can be compared readily with their standing on standardized tests of aptitude and achievement.

The nature of the stanine system.   The stanine scale is a system of standard scores that divides the distribution of raw scores into nine parts (the term *stanine* was derived from *standard nines*). The highest stanine score is 9, the lowest is 1, and stanine 5 is located precisely in the center of the distribution. Each stanine, except 1 and 9, includes a band of raw scores one half of a standard deviation wide. Thus, stanines are normally distributed standard scores with a mean of 5 and a standard deviation of 2. The percentage of a group that falls within each stanine in a normal distribution is as follows:

Stanine	1	2	3	4	5	6	7	8	9
Percentage	4	7	12	17	20	17	12	7	4

One of the greatest advantages of stanines is that we can apply them to any type of data that approximate a normal distribution and that can be ranked from high to low. We simply assign the top 4 percent of the students a stanine of 9, the next 7 percent a stanine of 8, and so on. To simplify this process, we can use tables such as Table 8.3 to determine the number of individuals in a group who should be assigned each stanine.

To use Table 8.3, all we need to do is enter the table with the size of the group with which we are working and, reading across the table, note the number of students who should be assigned each stanine score. For example, with a group of 30 students, one student would be assigned a stanine score of 1, two students a stanine score of 2, four students a stanine score of 3, and so on.

When raw scores are converted to stanines, they are in effect placed on a standard scale. This provides uniform meaning from one part of the scale to another and from one set of measures to another. Thus, the difference between a stanine of 7 and a stanine of 8 is the same as the difference between a stanine of 4 and a stanine of 5 or a stanine of 2 and a stanine of 3. This standard scale also makes it possible to compare relative standing on diverse types of measures. When stanines are all based on the same group of students, a particular stanine score refers to the same position in the group whether we are talking about scores on objective tests, essay ratings, oral reports, or a term paper. Thus, a stanine of 7 on each of these various measures would indicate the same distance above average. The simplicity of the system resides in the fact that we have standard units that can be expressed by a single digit. Since the mean score is always 5, relative standing within a set of scores and comparative standing on different sets of scores can be quickly grasped.

Probably the most useful function stanines serve is in the weighting and combining of diverse types of data for the purpose of obtaining a composite score, as in the determination of school marks. For example, let's assume that we have stanine scores for a mid-semester examination, laboratory work, and a final examination, and that we wish to give the first two equal weight and the final examination twice as much weight as either of the other two. For a student with the following stanine scores, then, our computation of a composite score would be as follows:

	STANINE		WEIGHT	WEIGHTED SCORE
Mid-semester examination	6	X	1	6
Laboratory work	4	X	1	4
Final examination	8	X	2	16
			Total = 26	

Composite score $= \dfrac{26}{4} = 6.5$

If composite scores were computed for each student in the group, these scores would provide a basis for ranking the students from high to low in terms of overall achievement. If final grades were to be assigned, the instructor would then simply

TABLE 8.3   Number of Individuals to be Assigned Each Stanine Score

	STANINES								
	1	2	3	4	5	6	7	8	9
SIZE OF GROUP	NUMBER OF INDIVIDUALS RECEIVING STANINE SCORE								
20	1	1	2	4	4	4	2	1	1
21	1	1	2	4	5	4	2	1	1
22	1	2	2	4	4	4	2	2	1
23	1	2	2	4	5	4	2	2	1
24	1	2	3	4	4	4	3	2	1
25	1	2	3	4	5	4	3	2	1
26	1	2	3	4	6	4	3	2	1
27	1	2	3	5	5	5	3	2	1
28	1	2	3	5	6	5	3	2	1
29	1	2	4	5	5	5	4	2	1
30	1	2	4	5	6	5	4	2	1
31	1	2	4	5	7	5	4	2	1
32	1	2	4	6	6	6	4	2	1
33	1	2	4	6	7	6	4	2	1
34	1	3	4	6	6	6	4	3	1
35	1	3	4	6	7	6	4	3	1
36	1	3	4	6	8	6	4	3	1
37	2	3	4	6	7	6	4	3	2
38	1	3	5	6	8	6	5	3	1
39	1	3	5	7	7	7	5	3	1
40	1	3	5	7	8	7	5	3	1
41	1	3	5	7	9	7	5	3	1
42	2	3	5	7	8	7	5	3	2
43	2	3	5	7	9	7	5	3	2
44	2	3	5	8	8	8	5	3	2
45	2	3	5	8	9	8	5	3	2
46	2	3	5	8	10	8	5	3	2
47	2	3	6	8	9	8	6	3	2
48	2	3	6	8	10	8	6	3	2
49	2	4	6	8	9	8	6	4	2
50	2	3	6	9	10	9	6	3	2
51	2	3	6	9	11	9	6	3	2
52	2	4	6	9	10	9	6	4	2
53	2	4	6	9	11	9	6	4	2
54	2	4	7	9	10	9	7	4	2
55	2	4	7	9	11	9	7	4	2
56	2	4	7	9	12	9	7	4	2
57	2	4	7	10	11	10	7	4	2
58	2	4	7	10	12	10	7	4	2
59	3	4	7	10	11	10	7	4	3
60	3	4	7	10	12	10	7	4	3

Note: If more than 60 students are in the group, see Gronlund (1985).

decide how many students should be given. As, how many Bs, how many Cs, and so on. Note that the composite score is not a stanine and that it does not tell us what grade should be assigned. It simply provides a ranking of students that accurately reflects the emphasis we wanted to give to each measure of achievement. The percentage of students to be assigned each letter grade is not a statistical decision but rather one that must be based on the educational level of the group, the ability of the students, the nature of the instruction, and the purposes to be served by the grades.

Assigning stanines to test scores.   If we wish to assign stanines to data that are in rank order and there are no ties in rank, we simply go down the ranked list and assign stanines in accordance with the distribution of stanine scores indicated in Table 8.3. When assigning stanines to test scores, however, we frequently have several students with the same raw score. Tie scores force us to deviate somewhat from the distribution in Table 8.3, since obviously *all students with the same raw score must be assigned the same stanine.* In assigning stanines to test scores, then, we try to approximate the theoretical distribution in Table 8.3 as closely as possible.

The steps to be followed in assigning stanines to test scores are listed as follows and illustrated by the data in Table 8.4. Note that the scores described in Table 8.4 are the same 30 test scores that were used earlier in this chapter.

1. Make a frequency distribution of scores. List every score from highest to lowest, and record in the frequency column the number of students who obtained each score (total number = 30 in Table 8.4).

TABLE 8.4   Assigning Stanines to a Frequency Distribution of Test Scores

STANINE	TEST SCORE	FREQUENCY	ACTUAL GROUPING	THEORETICAL GROUPING
9	38	1	1	1
8	37	1	1	2
	36	0		
7	35	2	5	4
	34	1		
	33	2		
6	32	3	5	5
	31	2		
5	30	1	7	6
	29	4		
	28	2		
4	27	2	4	5
	26	2		
3	25	3	4	4
	24	1		
	23	0		
2	22	1	2	2
	21	1		
1	20	0	1	1
	19	1		
		$N = 30$		

2. In the frequency column, count up from the bottom to the midpoint (median) of the set of scores (median = 29 in Table 8.4).

3. Enter the stanine table (Table 8.3) for a group size of 30 and determine the number of individuals to which a stanine of 5 should be assigned (six individuals). By going above and below the median, mark off as close to this number of scores (6) as possible (in Table 8.4, seven scores were included to keep stanine 5 centered).

4. By working up and down from stanine 5, assign raw scores to each stanine level so as to approximate the theoretical grouping (obtained from Table 8.3 and shown in Table 8.4) as closely as possible. If raw scores can be assigned to either of two stanines equally well, assign them to the stanine nearest the mean. In Table 8.4, for example, note that the two raw scores of 35 could be assigned to stanine 7 or stanine 8. They are assigned to stanine 7 in accordance with our rule.

5. When a tentative assignment has been completed, recheck to be certain that the actual grouping is as close to the theoretical distribution as possible. Then draw lines across the page, as shown in Table 8.4, and group the raw scores by stanine level.

STATISTICS FOR DESCRIBING A SET OF SCORES

For some purposes it is desirable to describe a set of scores in brief form. This is typically done by computing two measures: (1) the average score, or measure of *central tendency*, and (2) the spread of scores, or measure of *variability*.

Statisticians frown on the use of the term "average" in describing test scores because there are several different types of average. For a more precise description it is better to use the term which denotes the particular average being used. The three common types of averages are: (1) the *median*, or counting average, which is determined by arranging the scores in order of size and counting up to the midpoint of the series of scores, (2) the *mean*, or arithmetic average, which is determined by adding all of the scores in a set and dividing by the total number of scores, and (3) the *mode* or most frequently occurring score, which is determined simply by inspecting the frequency for each score. Of these types the median (commonly represented by *Mdn*) and the mean (commonly represented by M or $\overline{X}$) are most frequently used in describing the central tendency of a set of scores.

The spread, or variability, of a set of scores can be described in a number of different ways. Two of the more useful for decribing test scores are: (1) the *range*, which is simply the interval between the highest and lowest scores, and (2) the *standard deviation*, which is essentially an average of the degree to which the scores in a set deviate from the mean. Its meaning is most easily grasped by noting that a distance of one standard deviation above the mean and one standard deviation below the mean includes the range of approximately the middle two thirds of the scores (68 percent in a normal distribution). Thus, like the range for a set of scores, a large standard deviation indicates a big spread of scores (or great variability) and a smaller standard deviation indicates a smaller spread of scores (or less variability).

The standard deviation (*SD* or *s*) is an important and widely applicable statistic in testing. In addition to its use in describing the spread of scores in a group, it also serves as a basis for computing reliability coefficients, the standard error of measurement, and standard scores.

In describing test scores, the range may be used with the median or the mean. The standard deviation is used only with the mean.

Determining the Median and Range

The simplest method of describing a set of test scores is by using the median and the range.[2] These would be used where the group is small and where there is no need to compute further statistics. Thus, the data might be used to help students better understand their position in the group during class discussion and then be filed away or discarded.

To start with, the test scores should be arranged in rank order as shown in Table 8.5 (note that this is the same distribution of scores used in Tables 8.2 and 8.4). The median is then determined by locating the midpoint of the set of scores. This can be done by counting up from the bottom in the frequency column, to the point midway between the 15th and 16th score (15 scores are above this point and

TABLE 8.5 Frequency Distribution of Test Scores and Descriptive Statistics

TEST SCORE	FREQUENCY	
38	1	
37	1	
36	0	
35	2	
34	1	
33	2	
32	3	
31	2	
30	1	
29	4 ◄─────────── Median (estimated)	
28	2	
27	2	
26	2	
25	3	Median = 29
24	1	Range = 19
23	0	
22	1	Mean (rounded) = 29
21	1	Standard Deviation = 4.5
20	0	
19	1	
	$N = 30$	

[2]The quartile deviation can also be used with the median, but this is seldom used in describing test scores for classroom use. See a standard statistics book for its meaning and computation.

15 are below). In this case the midpoint falls at score 29, which is the median to the nearest whole number. Had the midpoint fallen between scores 29 and 30, the median would have been 29.5. With an odd number of scores the median always falls on an actual score because there is an equal number of scores above and below the middle score.[3]

The range of scores is determined by subtracting the lowest score from the highest score (sometimes 1 is added). In this case the range is 19 (38 − 19). Thus, this set of scores can be described as having a median of 29 and a range of 19 (ignore the mean and standard deviation for now). The median and range are terminal values: they are suitable for describing the scores in a small group, such as our group of 30 students, but they are not useful in computing further statistics.

The Mean, Standard Deviation, and Normal Curve

The mean and the standard deviation can probably best be understood in terms of the *normal curve*, although a normal distribution is not required for computing them. The normal curve is a symmetrical bell-shaped curve based on a precise mathematical equation. Scores distributed according to the normal curve are concentrated near the mean and decrease in frequency the further one departs from the mean. A sample normal curve is presented in Figure 8.3.

It will be noted in Figure 8.3 that the mean falls at the exact center of a normal distribution (the median and mode do also, but they are not relevant to our discussion). Note also that when the normal curve is divided into standard deviation (*SD*) units, which are equal distances along the baseline of the curve, each portion under the curve contains a fixed percentage of cases. Thus, 34 percent of the cases fall between the mean and +1 *SD*, 14 percent between +1 *SD* and +2 *SD*, and 2 percent between +2 *SD* and +3 *SD*. Since the curve is symmetrical, the same percentages, of course, apply to the intervals below the mean. These percentages have been rounded to the nearest whole number, but only a small fraction of a percent (0.13 percent) of the cases fall above and below three standard deviations from the mean. Thus, from a practical standpoint, a normal distribution of scores falls between −3 and +3 standard deviations from the mean.

To aid in understanding the meaning of standard deviation, a set of raw scores with a mean of 40 and a standard deviation of 5 has been placed below the baseline of the curve in Figure 8.3. Note that the mean raw score of 40 has been placed at the zero point and that the distance of one standard deviation is 5 raw score points everywhere along the baseline of the curve. Thus, the point one standard deviation above the mean equals 45 (40 + 5) and the point one standard deviation below the mean equals 35 (40 − 5). In this particular set of scores, then, approximately 68 percent of the scores (about two thirds) fall between 35 and 45, approximately 96 percent fall between 30 and 50, and approximately 99.7 percent fall between 25 and 55 (the figure shows 100 percent because numbers are rounded).

A simplified method for estimating the standard deviation for a set of scores

---

[3]More precise values of the median can be obtained with formulas found in standard statistics books, but these estimates are sufficiently precise for most classroom uses.

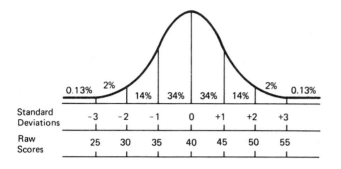

FIGURE 8.3.   Normal Curve with the Approximate Percentage of Cases Within Each Interval, (Percentages have been rounded).

will be described shortly. It is sufficient here to say that when the standard deviation is being computed for a set of normally distributed scores, we are essentially determining how far we need to go above (or below) the mean in raw score points to include 34 percent of the cases. Since the computed standard deviation for a particular set of scores has the same value everywhere along the baseline of the curve, it can be used along with the mean to describe the complete set of scores.

Determining the Mean and Standard Deviation

The mean and standard deviation are the preferred measures for analyzing and describing test scores. Unlike the median and range, which are determined by the midpoint and the two end scores, these statistics are based on the value of each score in the set. Thus, they provide more stable measures of central tendency and variability. An additional advantage is that these statistics are not terminal values, like the median and range, but can be used in making a number of other statistical computations useful in testing (such as reliability and standard scores).

The mean is obtained by adding all the scores in a set and dividing this sum by the number of scores. In Table 8.5, for example, the sum of the 30 separate scores is 872, and when this sum is divided by 30, a mean of 29.07 is obtained. You probably recognize this simple procedure, since the mean is the old arithmetic average that we all learned to compute in elementary school.

The standard deviation is a type of average of the amount that the scores differ from the mean. Basically it is obtained by determining how much each score deviates from the mean, squaring these deviations, summing the squared deviations, dividing by the number of scores, and then taking the square root. For classroom purposes it is usually satisfactory to use some simple method of estimating the standard deviation.

The simplest means of estimating the standard deviation is one presented in a bulletin by Diederich.[4] This procedure simply involves subtracting the sum of the

---

[4]P.B. Diederich, *Short-Cut Statistics for Teacher-Made Tests* (Princeton, N.J.: Educational Testing Service, 1973).

bottom sixth of scores from the sum of the top sixth and dividing by half the number of students in the group. Thus:

$$\text{Standard deviation } (SD) = \frac{\text{Sum of high sixth } - \text{ Sum of low sixth}}{\text{Half the number of students}}$$

In applying this formula to the set of scores in Table 8.5, we would add the top five scores (one sixth of 30) to obtain 179, add the bottom five scores to obtain 111, subtract the latter sum from the former, and divide the result by 15 (one half of 30) as follows:

$$SD = \frac{179 - 111}{15} = 4.53$$

Thus, the sample set of scores in Table 8.5 can be described as having a mean of 29 (rounded) and a standard deviation of 4.5 (rounded). Were this a normal distribution, we would expect about two thirds of the scores to fall between 24.5 (29 − 4.5) and 33.5 (29 + 4.5). Seventy percent of the scores in Table 8.5 fall within this range. With the scores from an informal classroom test, a perfectly normal distribution of scores is not to be expected. Such distributions of test scores frequently approximate a normal distribution closely enough, however, that the standard deviation can be used as a meaningful way of describing the spread of scores in the group.

A more efficient procedure for computing the standard deviation for use with a hand calculator is shown in the box.

Using z-Scores and T-Scores

A number of standard scores are based on the standard deviation unit. The simplest of these and the one that is basic to the others is the z-score. This score simply indicates, in standard deviation units, how far a given raw score is above or below the mean. The raw score of 45 in Figure 8.3, for example, would be assigned a z-score of 1.0 because it is one standard deviation above the mean. The raw score of 30 in Figure 8.3 would be given a z-score of −2.0 because it is two standard deviations below the mean. The formula for z-scores is:

$$z\text{-score} = \frac{\text{Raw score } - \text{ Mean}}{\text{Standard deviaion}}$$

For example, z-scores for raw scores of 47 and 36 in Figure 8.3 would be computed as follows:

$$z\text{-score} = \frac{47 - 40}{5} = 1.4 \qquad z\text{-score} = \frac{36 - 40}{5} = -.8$$

COMPUTATION OF THE STANDARD DEVIATION USING A HAND CALCULATOR

STEPS TO FOLLOW

1. Square each score in the set.
2. Add these squared values to obtain a total.
3. Divide the total by the number of scores in the set.
4. Square the mean of the set of scores.
5. Subtract the squared mean in step 4 from the result obtained in step 3.
6. Take the square root of the difference obtained in step 5. This is the standard deviation (*SD* or *s*).

FORMULA FOR THE COMPUTATIONAL STEPS

$$SD = \sqrt{\frac{\Sigma X^2 - M^2}{N}}$$

where Σ = "sum of"
X = a test score
N = number of scores
M = mean
$\sqrt{}$ = "square root of"

Thus, a raw score of 47 is 1.4 standard deviations above the mean and a raw score of 36 is .8 of a standard deviation below the mean.

While used in research, z-scores are seldom used directly in test interpretation because of the use of decimal points and minus signs. Instead, z-scores are converted to other types of standard scores that use only whole numbers and positive values. Such scores are more convenient to use and avoid the possibility of misinterpretation due to a forgotten minus sign.

Although many different types of standard scores are used with standardized tests, the T-score is one of the most commonly used with informal achievement tests. T-scores have a mean of 50 and a standard deviation of 10. They are obtained from z-scores by multiplying the z-score by 10 and adding the result of 50, as shown in the following formula.

T-score $= 50 + 10\ (z\text{-score})$

Applying the formula to the various z-scores discussed earlier (1.0, -2.0, 1.4, $-.8$) we would obtain T-scores as follows:

$T = 50 + 10\ (1.0) = 60 \qquad T = 50 + 10\ (-2.0) = 30$
$T = 50 + 10\ (1.4) = 64 \qquad T = 50 + 10\ (-.8)\ \ = 42$

T-scores can be easily interpreted because they always have the same mean and standard deviation. A *T*-score of 60 always means one standard deviation above the mean and a *T*-score of 30 always means two standard deviations below. Thus, with the use of *T*-scores, an individual's performance on different tests can be directly compared, and the scores can be combined or averaged without the distortion of different size standard deviations.

Where a normal distribution can be assumed, *T*-scores can also be interpreted in terms of percentile ranks because, in this case, there is a direct relationship between the two as shown in Figure 8.4. Note that a *T*-score of 30 is equivalent to a percentile rank of 2, a *T*-score of 40 is equivalent to a percentile rank of 16, and so on. This relationship will, of course, not hold if the distribution of raw scores is not normal because when this formula is used the distribution of *T*-scores retains the same shape as the distribution of raw scores. Although a non-normal distribution will limit the interpretation of *T*-scores in terms of percentile rank, their other valuable uses are retained (e.g., interpretation in terms of standard deviation units, and comparison and averaging of scores).

Because *T*-scores and percentile ranks both have a mean of 50 and use similar two-digit numbers, the two types of scores are often confused by those inexperienced in test interpretation. Thus, it is important to keep in mind that percentile rank indicates the percentage of individuals who fall at or below a given score, while a *T*-score indicates how many standard deviation units a given score falls above or below the mean. Note in Table 8.4 that although percentile ranks and *T*-scores have the same mean value of 50, below the mean percentile ranks are smaller than *T*-scores and above the mean they are larger than *T*-scores. This is accounted for, of course, by the fact that percentile ranks are crowded together in the center of the distribution and spread out at the ends, while *T*-scores provide equal units throughout the distribution of scores.

FIGURE 8.4. Corresponding Percentile Ranks, *z*-Scores, and *T*-Scores in a Normal Distribution.

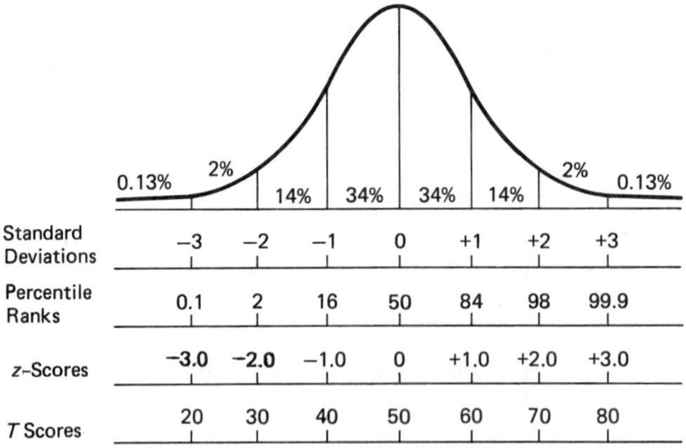

SUMMARY OF POINTS

The emphasis in this chapter can be summarized by the following points.

1. Test results can be interpreted in terms of the specific tasks that an individual can perform (criterion referenced), the individual's level of test performance in comparison to that of others (norm referenced), or both.

2. Criterion-referenced interpretation may be limited to a simple description of test performance (e.g., computes T-scores) or may include comparison to a performance standard (e.g., answers 80 percent of the items correctly).

3. Descriptions of test performance for instructional use may be improved by use of an item-response chart that indicates each individual's pattern of correct and incorrect responses.

4. Performance standards for test interpretation are arbitrarily set, but should be guided by the experience of the teacher, the nature of the group, the content of the test, and the degree to which the learning is essential to the next stage of instruction.

5. Norm-referenced interpretation involves comparing an individual's test score to the scores in some known group and indicating relative standing by means of simple ranking, percentile ranks, or some type of standard score.

6. A simple ranking of scores from high to low with a frequency column showing the number of individuals earning each score is satisfactory for presenting test results to small classroom groups.

7. A percentile rank indicates relative position in terms of the percentage of group members scoring at or below a given score. It should *not* be confused with the percentage of items answered correctly (a criterion-referenced interpretation).

8. Stanines are single-digit standard scores that range from a high of 9 to a low of 1, with a mean of 5. They are assigned by placing a given percentage of individuals in each stanine and are interpreted and used as standard scores.

9. A set of scores can be described by computing the average score (e.g., median or mean) and the variability, or spread, of scores (e.g., range or standard deviation).

10. The mean and standard deviation are especially useful statistics because they provide the basis for computing estimates of reliability and various types of standard scores (e.g., z-scores and T-scores).

11. A z-score simply indicates, in standard deviation units, how far a given raw score is above or below the mean.

12. A T-score indicates test performance in terms of a scale with a mean of 50 and a standard deviation of 10.

13. In a normal distribution there is a direct relationship between T-scores and percentile ranks, making it possible to interpret T-scores in terms of both types of score.

14. Because T-scores and percentile ranks both have a mean of 50 and use similar two-digit numbers, care must be taken not to confuse the two when interpreting test results.

ADDITIONAL READING

BERK, R. A., ED., *A Guide to Criterion-Referenced Test Construction* (Baltimore, Maryland: Johns Hopkins University Press, 1984). See Chapter 7 by L. A. Shepard, "Setting Performance Standards," for a review of methods and for guidelines for teacher-made classroom tests.

CRONBACH, L. J., *Essentials of Psychological Testing*, 4th ed. (New York: Harper & Row, 1984). See Chapter 4, "Scoring," for descriptions of various types of test scores and their interpretation.

GRONLUND, N. E., *Measurement and Evaluation in Teaching*, 5th ed. (New York: Macmillan Publishing Co., Inc., 1985). See Chapter 14, "Interpreting Test Scores and Norms," for a more comprehensive treatment of test scores and Appendix A, "Elementary Statistics," for a simplified treatment of statistical methods used in analyzing test scores.

JAEGER, R., *Statistics: A Spectator Sport* (Beverly Hills, CA: Sage Publications, 1983). Explains statistics, their uses and interpretation, with emphasis on understanding rather than computation.

LYMAN, H. B. *Test Scores and What They Mean*, 4th ed. (Englewood Cliffs, N.J.: Prentice-Hall, Inc., 1986) Clear, detailed, and easily grasped descriptions of the many types of scores used in testing.

9

Validity and Reliability

The two most important questions to ask about a test are: (1) To what extent will the interpretations of the scores be appropriate, meaningful, and useful? and (2) To what extent will the test scores be free from errors of measurement? . . . The first question is concerned with validity, the second with reliability . . . An understanding of both concepts is essential to effective test development and use.

Validity is the most important quality to consider in the preparation and use of achievement tests. First and foremost we want the test scores to serve their intended use. If we construct a test to measure a particular type of achievement, for example, we want the differences in test scores to reflect that particular type of achievement. Unless it does this to a satisfactory degree, the test is of little value and actually may be harmful if misinterpreted. Our second consideration is *reliability*, which refers to the consistency of our test results. If we tested individuals at a different time, or with a different sample of equivalent items, we would like to obtain approximately the same results. This consistency of results would indicate a low degree of measurement error, thus, giving us greater confidence that our test scores are accurate representations of the achievement being measured.

Although it is frequently unnecessary to make elaborate validation and reliability studies of informal achievement tests, an understanding of these concepts will contribute to skill in the construction, interpretation, and use of tests. Many of the essential elements of validity and reliability are built in during test development. Therefore, knowledge of validity and reliability provides a conceptual framework for building more effective tests. This knowledge also helps us avoid making inappropriate interpretations and improper applications when using test results.

VALIDITY

The meaning of validity has typically been defined for the testing profession by a set of *Standards* (1985) prepared by a joint committee made up of members selected from three leading professional organizations concerned with testing (American Educational Research Association, American Psychological Association, and The National Council on Measurement in Education). In the most recent edition of the *Standards*, validity has been described as follows:

> Validity is the most important consideration in test evaluation. The concept refers to the appropriateness, meaningfulness, and usefulness of the specific inferences made from test scores. Test validation is the process of accumulating evidence to support such inferences. A variety of inferences may be made from scores produced by a given test, and there are many ways of accumulating evidence to support any particular inference. Validity, however, is a unitary concept. Although evidence may be accumulated in many ways, validity always refers to the degree to which that evidence supports the inferences that are made from the scores. The inferences regarding specific uses of a test are validated, not the test itself.

This brief description of validity includes a number of important points and one very significant change concerning the conceptual nature of validity. These points are listed here to further clarify the meaning of validity.

1. Validity is *inferred* from available evidence (not measured).
2. Validity depends on *many different types* of evidence.
3. Validity is expressed by *degree* (high, moderate, low).
4. Validity is *specific* to a particular use.
5. Validity refers to the *inferences drawn*, not the test itself.
6. Validity is a *unitary concept.*

Describing validity as a unitary concept is a basic change in how validity is viewed. The traditional view that there were several different "types of validity" has been replaced by the view that validity is a single, unitary concept that is based on various forms of evidence. The former "types of validity" (content, criterion related, and construct) are now simply considered to be convenient categories for accumulating evidence to support the validity of an interpretation. Thus, we no longer speak of "content validity," but of "content-related evidence" of validity. Similarly, we speak of "criterion-related evidence" and "construct-related evidence" (see Figure 9.1).

For some interpretations of test scores only one or two types of evidence may be critical, but an *ideal* validation would include evidence from all three categories. We are most likely to draw valid inferences from test scores when we have a full understanding of: (1) the nature of the test content and the specifications that were used in developing the test, (2) the relation of the test scores to significant criterion measures, and (3) the nature of the psychological characteristic(s) or construct(s) being measured by the test. Although in many practical situations the evidence falls

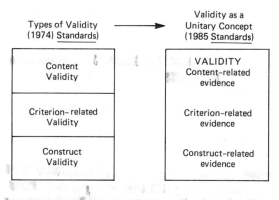

FIGURE 9.1. Illustration of Shift from "Types of Validity" to "Validity as a Unitary Concept"

short of this ideal, we should gather as much relevant evidence as is feasible within the constraints of the situation.

The various approaches to test validation and the question to be answered by each are summarized in Table 9.1.

Content-Related Evidence

Content-related evidence of validity is critical when we want to use test performance as evidence of performance in a larger domain of content. Let's assume, for example, that we have a list of 500 words that we expect our students to be able to spell correctly at the end of the school year. To test their spelling ability, we might give them a 50-word spelling test. Their performance on these words is important only insofar as it provides evidence of their ability to spell the 500 words. Thus, our spelling test would provide a valid measure to the degree to which it provided an adequate sample of the 500 words it represented. If we selected only easy words, only difficult words, or only words that represented certain types of common spelling errors, our test would tend to be unrepresentative and thus have

TABLE 9.1 Basic Approaches to Test Validation

TYPE OF EVIDENCE	QUESTION TO BE ANSWERED
Content-Related Evidence	How adequately does the sample of test items represent the domain of content to be measured?
Criterion-Related Evidence	How accurately does test performance predict future performance (predictive study) or estimate present performance (concurrent study) on some other valued measure called a *criterion*?
Construct-Related Evidence	How well can test performance be explained in terms of psychological characteristics?

low validity. If we selected a balanced sample of words that took these and similar factors into account, our test would provide a representative measure of the 500 spelling words.

It should be clear from this discussion that the key element in content-related evidence of validity is the adequacy of the *sampling.* A test is always a sample of the many questions that could be asked. Content validation is a matter of determining whether the sample is representative of the larger domain of content it is supposed to represent.

Content-related evidence of validity is especially important in achievement testing. Here we are interested in how well the test measures the intended learning outcomes of the instruction. We can build a test that has high validity by (1) identifying the learning outcomes to be measured, (2) preparing a test plan that specifies the sample of items to be used, and (3) constructing a test that closely fits the set of test specifications. These are the best procedures we have for ensuring the measurement of a representative sample of the intended learning outcomes. Note that these procedures are the same ones we have described in considerable detail in earlier chapters. Thus, we have been concerned with constructing valid tests throughout this book, even though we have not identified it as such.

The makers of standardized tests follow these same systematic procedures in building achievement tests, but the content and learning outcomes included in the test specifications are more broadly based. Typically, they are based on the leading textbooks and the recommendations of various experts in the area being covered by the test. Therefore, a standardized achievement test may be representative of a broad range of content but be unrepresentative of the domain of content taught in a particular school situation. To determine relevance to the local situation, it is necessary to evaluate the sample of test items in light of the content and skills emphasized in the instruction.

In summary, content-related evidence of validity is of major concern in achievement testing, whether you are developing or selecting a test. When constructing a test, content relevance and representativeness are built in by following a systematic procedure for specifying and selecting the sample of test items. In test selection, it is a matter of comparing the test sample to the domain of content to be measured and determining the degree of correspondence between them. Thus, content-related evidence of validity is obtained primarily by careful logical analysis.

Criterion-Related Evidence

There are two types of studies used in obtaining criterion-related evidence of validity. The first is concerned with the use of test performance to predict future performance on some other valued measure called a *criterion.* For example, we might use scholastic aptitude test scores to predict course grades (the criterion). For obvious reasons, this is called a *predictive* study. The second type of study is concerned with the use of test performance to estimate current performance on some criterion. For instance, we might want to use a test of study skills to estimate what the outcome would be of a careful observation of students in an actual study situation (the criterion). Since with this procedure both measures (test and criterion) are obtained at approximately the same time, this type of study is called a *concurrent* study.

Although the value of using a predictive study is rather obvious, a question might be raised concerning the purpose of a concurrent study. Why would anyone want to use test scores to estimate performance on some other measure that is to be obtained at the same time? There are at least three good reasons for doing this. First, we may want to check the results of a newly constructed test against some existing test that has a considerable amount of validity evidence supporting it. Second, we may want to substitute a brief, simple testing procedure for a more complex and time-consuming measure. For example, our test of study skills might be substituted for an elaborate rating system if it provided a satisfactory estimate of study performance. Third, we may want to determine whether a testing procedure has *potential* as a predictive instrument. If a test provides an unsatisfactory estimate of current performance, it certainly cannot be expected to predict future performance on the same measure. On the other hand, a satisfactory estimate of present performance would indicate that the test may be useful in predicting future performance as well. This would inform us that a predictive study would be worth doing.

The key element in both types of criterion-related study is the *degree of relationship* between the two sets of measures: (1) the test scores, and (2) the criterion to be predicted or estimated. This relationship is typically expressed by means of a correlation coefficient or an expectancy table.

Correlation Coefficients.   Although the computation of correlation coefficients is beyond the scope of this book, the concept of correlation can easily be grasped. A correlation coefficient (*r*) simply indicates the degree of relationship between two sets of measures. A positive relationship is indicated when high scores on one measure are accompanied by high scores on the other; low scores on the two measures are similarly associated. A *negative* relationship is indicated when high scores on one measure are accompanied by low scores on the other measure. The extreme degrees of relationship it is possible to obtain between two sets of scores are indicated by the following values:

$$1.00 = \text{perfect positive relationship}$$
$$.00 = \text{no relationship}$$
$$-1.00 = \text{perfect negative relationship}$$

When a correlation coefficient is used to express the degree of relationship between a set of test scores and some criterion measure, it is called a *validity coefficient*. For example, a validity coefficient of 1.00 applied to the relationship between a set of aptitude test scores (the predictor) and a set of achievement test scores (the criterion) would indicate that each individual in the group had exactly the same relative standing on both measures, and would thereby provide a perfect prediction from the aptitude scores to the achievement scores. Most validity coefficients are smaller than this, but the extreme positive relationship provides a useful bench mark for evaluating validity coefficients. The closer the validity coefficient approaches 1.00, the higher the degree of relationship and, thus, the more accurate our predictions of each individual's success on the criterion will be.

A more realistic procedure for evaluating a validity coefficient is to compare it to the validity coefficients that are *typically* obtained when the two measures are correlated. For example, a validity coefficient of .40 between a set of aptitude test scores and achievement test scores would be considered small because we typically obtain coefficients in the .50 to .70 range for these two measures. Therefore, validity coefficients must be judged on a relative basis, the larger coefficients being favored. To use validity coefficients effectively, one must become familiar with the size of the validity coefficients that are typically obtained between various pairs of measures.

Expectancy Table.   The expectancy table is a simple and practical means of expressing criterion-related evidence of validity and is especially useful for making predictions from test scores. The expectancy table is simply a twofold chart with the test scores (the predictor) arranged in categories down the left side of the table and the measure to be predicted (the criterion) arranged in categories across the top of the table. For each category of scores on the *predictor*, the table indicates the percentage of individuals who fall within each category of the *criterion*. An example of an expectancy table is presented in Table 9.2.

Note in Table 9.2 that of those students who were in the above-average group (stanines 7, 8, and 9) on the test scores, 43 percent received a grade of A, 43 percent a B, and 14 percent a C. Although these percentages are based on this particular group, it is possible to use them to predict the future performance of other students in this science course. Hence, if a student falls in the above-average group on this scholastic aptitude test, we might predict that he or she has 43 chances out of 100 of earning an A, 43 chances out of 100 of earning a B, and 14 chances out of a 100 of earning a C in this particular science course. Such predictions are highly tentative, of course, due to the small number of students on which this expectancy table was

TABLE 9.2   Expectancy Table Showing the Relation Between Scholastic Aptitude Scores and Course Grades for 30 Students in a Science Course

GROUPED SCHOLASTIC APTITUDE SCORES (STANINES)	PERCENTAGE IN EACH SCORE CATEGORY RECEIVING EACH GRADE				
	E	D	C	B	A
Above Average (7, 8, 9)			14	43	43
Average (4, 5, 6)		19	37	25	19
Below Average (1, 2, 3)	57	29	14		

built. Teachers can construct more dependable tables by accumulating data from several classes over a period of time.

Expectancy tables can be used to show the relationship between any two measures. Constructing the table is simply a matter of (1) grouping the scores on each measure into a series of categories (any number of them), (2) placing the two sets of categories on a twofold chart, (3) tabulating the number of students who fall into each position in the table (based on the student's standing on both measures), and (4) converting these numbers to percentages (of the total number in that row). Thus, the expectancy table is a clear way of showing the relationship between sets of scores. Although the expectancy table is more cumbersome to deal with than a correlation coefficient, it has the special advantage of being easily understood by persons without knowledge of statistics. Thus, it can be used in practical situations to clarify the predictive efficiency of a test.

Construct-Related Evidence

The construct-related category of evidence focuses on test performance as a basis for inferring the possession of certain psychological characteristics. For example, we might want to describe a person's reading comprehension, reasoning ability, or mechanical aptitude. These are all hypothetical qualities, or *constructs*, that we assume exist in order to explain behavior. Such theoretical constructs are useful in describing individuals and in predicting how they will act in many different specific situations. To describe a person as being highly intelligent, for example, is useful because that term carries with it a series of associated meanings that indicate what the individual's behavior is likely to be under various conditions. Before we can interpret test scores in terms of these broad behavior descriptions, however, we must first establish that the constructs that are presumed to be reflected in the test scores actually do account for differences in test performance.

Construct-related evidence of validity includes (1) a description of the theoretical framework that specifies the nature of the construct to be measured, (2) a description of the development of the test and any aspects of measurement that may affect the meaning of the test scores (e.g., test format), (3) the pattern of relationship between the test scores and other significant variables (e.g., high correlations with similar tests and low correlations with tests measuring different constructs), and (4) any other type of evidence that contributes to the meaning of the test scores (e.g., analyzing the mental process used in responding, determining the predictive effectiveness of the test). The specific types of evidence that are most critical for a particular test depend on the nature of the construct, the clarity of the theoretical framework, and the uses to be made of the test scores. Although the gathering of construct-related evidence of validity can be endless, in practical situations it is typically necessary to limit the evidence to that which is most relevant to the interpretations to be made.

The construct-related category of evidence is the broadest of the three categories. Evidence obtained in both the content-related category (e.g., representativeness of the sample of items) and the criterion-related category (e.g., how well the test scores predict performance on specific criteria) are also relevant to the construct-related category because they help to clarify the meaning of the test scores. Thus, the construct-related category encompasses a variety of types of evidence, including that from content-related and criterion-related validation studies. (See figure 9.2.)

The broad array of evidence that might be considered can be illustrated by a test designed to measure mathematical reasoning ability. Some of the evidence we might consider is as follows:

1. Compare the sample of test tasks to the domain of tasks specified by the conceptual framework of the construct. Is the sample relevant and representative (content-related evidence)?
2. Examine the test features and their possible influence on the meaning of the scores (e.g., test format, directions, scoring, reading level of items). Is it possible that some features might distort the scores?
3. Analyze the mental process used in answering the questions by having students "think aloud" as they respond to each item. Do the items require the intended reasoning process?
4. Determine the internal consistency of the test by intercorrelating the test items. Do the items seem to be measuring a single characteristic (in this case mathematical reasoning)?
5. Correlate the test scores with the scores of other mathematical reasoning tests. Do they show a high degree of relationship?
6. Compare the scores of known groups (e.g., mathematics majors and nonmajors). Do the scores differentiate between the groups as predicted?
7. Compare the scores of students before and after specific training in mathematical reasoning. Do the scores change as predicted from the theory underlying the construct?
8. Correlate the scores with grades in mathematics. Do they correlate to a satisfactory degree (criterion-related evidence)?

Other types of evidence could be added to this list but it is sufficiently comprehensive to make clear that no single type of evidence is adequate. Interpreting test scores as a measure of a particular construct involves a comprehensive study

FIGURE 9.2. Construct Validation Includes All Categories of Evidence.

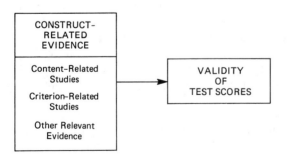

of the development of the test, how it functions in a variety of situations, and how the test scores relate to other significant measures.

Test scores are, of course, influenced by many factors other than the construct the test is designed to measure. Thus, construct validation is an attempt to account for all possible influences on the scores. We might, for example, ask to what extent the scores on our mathematical reasoning test are influenced by reading comprehension, computation skill, and speed. Each of these factors would require further study. Were attempts made to eliminate such factors during test development by using simple vocabulary, simple computations and liberal time limits? To what extent do the test scores correlate with measures of reading comprehension and computational skill? How do students' scores differ under different time limits? Answers to these and similar questions will help us to determine how well the test scores reflect the construct we are attempting to measure and the extent to which other factors might be influencing the scores.

Construct validation, then, is an attempt to clarify and verify the inferences to be made from the test scores. This involves a wide variety of procedures and many different types of evidence (including both content-related and criterion-related evidence). As evidence accumulates from many different sources, our interpretations of the test scores are enriched and we are able to make them with greater confidence.

METHODS OF DETERMINING RELIABILITY

Reliability refers to the *consistency* of test scores—that is, to how consistent they are from one measurement to another. Because of the ever present errors of measurement, we can expect a certain amount of variation in test performance from one time to another, from one sample of items to another, and from one part of the test to another. Reliability measures provide an estimate of how much variation we might expect under different conditions. The reliability of test scores is typically reported by means of a *reliability coefficient* or the *standard error of measurement* that is derived from it. Since both methods of estimating reliability require score variability, the procedures to be discussed are useful primarily with norm-referenced tests.

As we noted earlier, a correlation coefficient expressing the relationship between a set of test scores and a criterion measure is called a validity coefficient. A reliability coefficient is also a correlation coefficient, but it indicates the correlation between two sets of measurements taken from the same procedure. We may, for example, administer the same test twice to a group, with a time interval in between (*test-retest* method); administer two equivalent forms of the test in close succession (*equivalent-forms* method); administer two equivalent forms of the test with a time interval in between (*test-retest* with *equivalent forms* method); or administer the test once and compute the consistency of the responses within the test (*internal-consistency* method). Each of these methods of obtaining reliability provides a different type of information (American Psychological Association, 1985). Thus, reliability coefficients obtained with the different procedures are not interchangeable. Before deciding on the procedure to be used, we must determine what type of reliability evidence we are seeking. The four basic methods of estimating reliability and the type of information each provides are shown in Table 9.3.

Test-Retest Method

The test-retest method requires administering the same form of the test to the same group after some time interval. The time between the two administrations may be just a few days or several years. The length of the time interval should fit the type of interpretation to be made from the results. Thus, if we are interested in using test scores only to group students for more effective learning, short-term stability may be sufficient. On the other hand, if we are attempting to predict vocational success or make some other long-range predictions, we would desire evidence of stability over a period of years.

Test-retest reliability coefficients are influenced both by errors within the measurement procedure and by the day-to-day stability of the students' responses. Thus, longer time periods between testing will result in lower reliability coefficients, due to the greater changes in the students. In reporting test-retest reliability coefficients, then, it is important to include the time interval. For example, a report might state: "The stability of test scores obtained on the same form over a three-month period was .90." This makes it possible to determine the extent to which the reliability data are significant for a particular interpretation.

Equivalent-Forms Method

With this method, two equivalent forms of a test (also called alternate forms or parallel forms) are administered to the same group during the same testing session. The test forms are equivalent in the sense that they are built to measure the same abilities (that is, they are built to the same set of specifications), but for

TABLE 9.3   Methods of Estimating Reliability

METHOD	TYPE OF INFORMATION PROVIDED
Test-retest method	The stability of test scores over a given period of time.
Equivalent-forms method	The consistency of the test scores over different forms of the test (that is, different samples of items).
Test-retest with equivalent forms	The consistency of test scores over *both* a time interval and different forms of the test.
Internal-consistency methods	The consistency of test scores over different parts of the test.

Note: Scorer reliability should also be considered when evaluating the responses to *supply-type* items (for example, essay tests). This is typically done by having the test papers scored independently by two scorers and then correlating the two sets of scores. Agreement among scorers, however, is not a substitute for the methods of estimating reliability shown in the table.

determining reliability it is also important that they be constructed independently. When this is the case, the reliablity coefficient indicates the adequacy of the test sample. That is, a high reliability coefficient would indicate that the two independent samples are apparently measuring the same thing. A low reliability coefficient, of course, would indicate that the two forms are measuring different behavior and that therefore both samples of items are questionable.

Reliability coefficients determined by this method take into account errors within the measurement procedure and consistency over different samples of items, but they do not include the day-to-day stability of the students' responses.

Test-Retest Method with Equivalent Forms

This is a combination of both methods. Here, two different forms of the same test are administered with time intervening. This is the most demanding estimate of reliability, since it takes into account all possible sources of variation. The reliability coefficient reflects errors within the testing procedure, consistency over different samples of items, and the day-to-day stability of the students' responses. For most purposes, this is probably the most useful type of reliability, since it enables us to estimate how generalizable the test results are over the various conditions. A high reliability coefficient obtained by this method would indicate that a test score represents not only present test performance but also what test performance is likely to be at another time or on a different sample of equivalent items.

Internal-Consistency Methods

These methods require only a single administration of a test. One procedure, the *split-half* method, involves scoring the odd items and the even items separately and correlating the two sets of scores. This correlation coefficient indicates the degree to which the two arbitrarily selected halves of the test provide the same results. Thus, it reports on the internal consistency of the test. Like the equivalent-forms method, this procedure takes into account errors within the testing procedure and consistency over different samples of items, but it omits the day-to-day stability of the students' responses.

Since the correlation coefficient based on the odd and even items indicates the relationship between two halves of the test, the reliability coefficient for the total test is determined by applying the Spearman-Brown prophecy formula. A simplified version of this formula is as follows:

$$\text{Reliability of total test} = \frac{2 \times \text{reliability for } \frac{1}{2} \text{ test}}{1 + \text{reliability for } \frac{1}{2} \text{ test}}$$

Thus, if we obtained a correlation coefficient of .60 for two halves of a test, the reliability for the total test would be computed as follows:

$$\text{Reliability of total test} = \frac{2 \times .60}{1 + .60} = \frac{1.20}{1.60} = .75$$

This application of the Spearman-Brown formula makes clear a useful principle of test reliability; the realiability of a test can be increased by lengthening it. This formula shows how much reliability will increase when the length of the test is doubled. Application of the formula, however, assumes that the test is lengthened by adding items like those already in the test.

Probably the simplest means of estimating the reliability of test scores from a single administration of a test is to use Kuder-Richardson Formula 21. This formula requires just three types of information: (1) the number of items in the test, (2) the mean (or arithmetic average), and (3) the standard deviation. Since we learned a short-cut method for estimating the standard deviation in the last chapter, this formula is especially easy to apply to classroom achievement tests. A simplified version of the formula follows. Although this formula omits a mirror correction factor, it is satisfactory for use with most classroom tests.

$$\text{Reliability estimate } (KR21) = 1 - \frac{M(K - M)}{K(s^2)}$$

where K = the number of items in the test; M = the mean of the test scores; and s = the standard deviatioin of the test scores.

Although this formula may look a bit formidable at first glance, we simply insert the quantities called for and apply our arithmetic skills. For example, if K = 40, M = 29, and s = 4.5 (from the data in Table 8.5), the reliability estimate would be computed as follows:

$$\text{Reliability} = 1 - \frac{29\ (40 - 29)}{40(4.5^2)}$$

$$= 1 - \frac{29 \times 11}{40 \times 20.25}$$

$$= 1 - .39$$

$$= .61$$

Thus, the reliability estimate for our 40-item test is .61. We might now ask if the reliability of these test scores is high or low. As with validity coefficients, there are two readily usable bench marks for evaluating a reliability coefficient. First, we can compare it with the extreme degrees of reliability that it is possible to obtain. A complete lack of reliability would be indicated by a coefficient of .00, and perfect positive reliability would be indicated by a coefficient of 1.00. This provides a general framework within which to view a particular reliability coefficient. Second, and probably more important, we can compare our reliability coefficient with those that are usually obtained for achievement tests. The reported reliabilities for standardized achievement tests are frequently over .90 when Kuder-Richardson formulas are used. The reliability coefficients for classroom tests typically range between .60 and .80. When we view our reliability coefficient in this light, we might consider it to be rather low.

Kuder-Richardson formula 21 provides a conservative estimate of reliability. Since it is based on the consistency of student response from item to item, it tends to provide smaller correlation coefficients than the split-half method.

Internal-consistency methods are used because they require that the test be administered only once. They should not be used with speeded tests, however, because a spuriously high reliability estimate will result. If speed is an important factor in the testing (that is, if the students do not have time to attempt all the items), other methods should be used to estimate reliability.

Standard Error of Measurement

The standard error of measurement is an especially useful way of expressing test reliability because it indicates the amount of error to allow for when interpreting individual test scores. The standard error is derived from a reliability coefficient by means of the following formula:

$$\text{Standard error of measurement} = s \sqrt{1 - r_{tt}}$$

where s = the standard deviation and r_{tt} = the reliability coefficient. In applying this formula to the Kuder-Richardson reliability estimate of .61 obtained earlier ($s = 4.5$), the following results would be obtained.

$$\text{Standard error of measurement} = 4.5 \sqrt{1 - .61}$$

$$= 4.5 \sqrt{.39}$$

$$= 4.5 \times .63$$

$$= 2.8$$

Although the standard error of measurement is easily computed, for most informal achievement testing a satisfactory approximation of this measure can be obtained from the length of the test. The table on page 148, prepared by Paul Diederich,[1] provides an estimate of the amount of error to be expected in tests of different lengths. The standard-error column shows how many points we must add to, and subtract from, an individual's test score in order to obtain "reasonable limits" for estimating that individual's true score (that is, a score free of error).

If we were using a 40-item test, as in our earlier example, the standard error would be approximately 3 score points. Thus, if a given student scored 35 on this test, that student's *score band*, for establishing reasonable limits, would range from 32 (35 − 3) to 38 (35 + 3). In other words, we could be reasonably sure that the score band of 32 to 38 included the student's true score (statistically, there are two chances out of three that it does). These estimated standard errors of test scores

[1]P. B. Diederich, *Short-Cut Statistics for Teacher-Made Tests* (Princeton, N.J.: Educational Testing Service, 1973).

NUMBER OF ITEMS IN THE TEST	STANDARD ERROR
less than 24	2
24-47	3
48-89	4
90-109	5
110-129	6
130-150	7

provide a rough indication of the amount of error to expect in tests of different lengths, and they highlight the importance of allowing for error during test interpretation. If we view test performance in terms of score bands (also called *confidence bands*), we are not likely to overinterpret small differences between test scores.

The previous table also illustrates that the proportionate amount of error in a test score becomes smaller as the test becomes longer. Note, for example, that a test of 50 items has a standard error of 4 and a test of 100 items has a standard error of 5. Although the length of the test is doubled, the amount of error is increased by only one fourth. This is in harmony with the principle stated earlier: longer tests provide more reliable results.

For the test user, the standard error of measurement is probably more useful than the reliability coefficient. Although reliability coefficients can be used in evaluating the quality of a test and in comparing the relative merits of different tests, the standard error of measurement is directly applicable to the interpretation of individual test scores.

Reliability of Criterion-Referenced Mastery Tests

As noted earlier, the traditional methods for computing reliability require score variability (that is, a spread of scores) and are therefore useful mainly with norm-referenced tests. When used with criterion-referenced tests, they are likely to provide misleading results. Since criterion-referenced tests are not designed to emphasize differences among individuals, they typically have limited score variability. This restricted spread of scores will result in low correlation estimates of reliability, even if the consistency of our test results is adequate for the use to be made of them.

When a criterion-referenced test is used to determine mastery (which is its major use), our primary concern is with how consistently our test classifies masters and nonmasters. If we administered two equivalent forms of a test to the same group of students, for example, we would like the results of both forms to identify the same students as having mastered the material. Such perfect agreement is unrealistic, of course, since some students near the cut-off score are likely to shift from one category to the other on the basis of errors of measurement (due to such factors as lucky guesses or lapses of memory). However, if too many students demonstrated mastery on one form but nonmastery on the other, our decisions concerning who mastered the material would be hopelessly confused. Thus, the reliability of mastery tests can be determined by computing the percentage of consistent mastery-nonmastery decisions over the two forms of the test.

The procedure for comparing test performance on two equivalent forms of a test is relatively simple. After both forms have been administered to a group of students, the resulting data can be placed in a two-by-two table like that shown in Figure 9.3.

| | FORM B | |
	NONMASTERS	MASTERS
MASTERS (FORM A)	2	30
NONMASTERS	6	2

FIGURE 9.3. Classification of Forty Students as Masters or Nonmasters on Two Forms of a Criterion-Referenced Test.

These data are based on two forms of a 25-item test administered to 40 students. Mastery was set at 80 percent correct (20 items), so all students who scored 20 or higher on both forms of the test were placed in the upper right-hand cell (30 students), and all those who scored below 20 on both forms were placed in the lower left-hand cell (6 students). The remaining students demonstrated mastery on one form and nonmastery on the other (4 students). Since 36 of the 40 students were consistently classified by the two forms of the test, we apparently have reasonably good consistency.

We can compute the percentage of consistency for this procedure with the following formula:

$$\% \text{ Consistency} = \frac{\text{Masters (both forms)} + \text{Nonmasters (both forms)}}{\text{Total number in group}} \times 100$$

$$\% \text{ Consistency} = \frac{30 + 6}{40} \times 100 = 90\%$$

This procedure is simple to use but it has a few limitations. First, two forms of the test are required. This may not be as serious as it seems, however, since in most mastery programs more than one form of the test is needed for retesting those students who fail to demonstrate mastery on the first try. Second, it is difficult to determine what percentage of decision consistency is necessary for a given situation. As with other measures of reliability, the greater the consistency, the more satisfied we will be, but what constitutes a minimum acceptable level? There is no simple answer to such a question because it depends on the number of items in the test and the consequences of the decision. If a nonmastery decision for a student simply means further study and later retesting, low consistency might be acceptable. However, if the mastery-nonmastery decision concerns whether to give a student a high school certificate, as in some competency testing programs, then a high level of consistency will be demanded. Since there are no clear guidelines for setting minimum levels, we will need to depend on experience in various situations to determine what are reasonable expectations.

More sophisticated techniques have been developed for estimating the reliability of criterion-referenced tests, but the numerous issues and problems involved in their use go beyond the scope of this book. For detailed discussions of recent developments see R. A. Berk (1984) in the Additional Reading list at the end of the chapter.

SUMMARY OF POINTS

The emphasis in this chapter can be summarized by the following points.

1. Validity is the most important quality to consider in testing and "refers to the appropriateness, meaningfulness, and usefulness of the specific inferences made from test scores" (*Standards*, 1985).
2. Validity is a *unitary concept* based on various forms of evidence (content-related, criterion-related, and construct-related evidence).
3. Content-related evidence of validity refers to how well the sample of test items represents the domain of content to be measured.
4. Content-related evidence of validity is of major concern in achievement testing and is "built in" by following systematic procedures during test construction.
5. Criterion-related evidence of validity refers to the degree to which test scores are related to some other valued measure called a *criterion*.
6. Criterion-related evidence may be based on a predictive study or a concurrent study and is typically expressed by a correlation coefficient or expectancy table.
7. Construct-related evidence of validity refers to how well test performance can be explained in terms of psychological characteristics, or constructs (e.g., mathematical reasoning).
8. The construct-related category of evidence is the most comprehensive. It includes evidence from both content-related and criterion-related studies plus other types of evidence that help clarify the meaning of the test scores.
9. Reliability refers to the consistency of test scores (i.e., to the degree to which the scores are free from errors of measurement).
10. Reliability of test scores is typically reported by means of a reliability coefficient or a standard error of measurement.
11. Reliability coefficients can be obtained by a number of different methods (e.g., test-retest, equivalent-forms, internal-consistency) and each one measures a different type of consistency (e.g., over time, over different samples of items, over different parts of the test).

12. The standard error of measurement indicates the amount of error to allow for when interpreting individual test scores.

13. Score bands (or *confidence bands*) take into account the error of measurement and help prevent the overinterpretation of small differences between test scores.

14. The reliability of criterion-referenced mastery tests can be obtained by computing the percentage of agreement between two forms of the test in classifying individuals as masters and nonmasters.

ADDITIONAL READING

AMERICAN PSYCHOLOGICAL ASSOCIATION, *Standards for Educational and Psychological Testing* (Washington, D.C.: APA, 1985). See the sections on validity (pages 9–18) and reliability (pages 19–23) for descriptions of the concepts and sets of standards.

BERK, R. A., ED., *A Guide to Criterion-Referenced Test Construction* (Baltimore, Maryland: Johns Hopkins University Press, 1984). See Chapter 8 by R. K. Hambleton, "Validating the Test Scores," and Chapter 9 by R. A. Berk, "Selecting the Index of Reliability," for reviews of methods used with criterion-referenced tests.

CRONBACH, L. J. *Essentials of Psychological Testing*, 4th ed. (New York: Harper & Row, 1984). Chapters 5 and 6. Describes and illustrates the procedures for determining the validity and reliability of test scores.

GRONLUND, N. E., *Measurement and Evaluation in Teaching*, 5th ed. (New York: Macmillan Publishing Co., Inc., 1985). Chapters 3 and 4. The procedures for determining validity and reliability are described and illustrated, with emphasis on educational testing. Written to reflect the 1985 APA *Standards*.

Appendix

Checklist for evaluating informal

achievement tests

The following checklist was designed to aid in evaluating the quality of informal achievement tests. The questions are phrased so that they apply to both norm-referenced and criterion-referenced tests, and a "yes" answer indicates that the criterion has been met. A negative answer to any question indicates an error in construction that should be corrected. A review of the items in the checklist before starting test construction can provide a useful procedure for avoiding errors during construction.

TEST SPECIFICATIONS

1. Do the test specifications describe the nature and limits of the achievement domain to be measured?
2. Are the intended learning outcomes stated in performance (measurable) terms?
3. Do the test specifications indicate the nature and distribution of items to be included in the test?
4. If mastery standards are set, is justification given for the cut-off scores?

TEST FORMAT AND DIRECTIONS

1. Does the item arrangement on the page contribute to ease of reading and responding?
2. Are items of the same type placed together in the test (to minimize the number of directions needed)?
3. Are the items arranged in order of increasing difficulty within each section of the test?

4. Do the method of answering and the location of the answer space contribute to efficient test taking?
5. Are the items numbered in consecutive order throughout the test?
6. Is there a balanced proportion of correct answers (that is, A, B, C, D) and is the sequence of answers free of patterning (that is, A, B, A, B)?
7. Are clear and concise directions provided for the test as a whole and for each separate section?
8. Is the final copy of the test satisfactory in terms of spacing, legibility, and freedom from errors?

TEST ITEMS

A. General

1. Is each test item relevant to an important learning outcome?
2. Is each item type appropriate for the particular learning outcome to be measured?
3. Does each item present a clearly formulated task?
4. Is each item stated in simple, clear language and free of nonfunctional material?
5. Is each item free of extraneous clues?
6. Is the difficulty of each item appropriate for the task and for the use to be made of the results?
7. Is the answer to each item one that would be agreed upon by experts?
8. Is there an adequate number of items for each interpretation to be made?
9. Are the items sufficiently independent that one item does not aid in answering another?
10. Are the items free from race, ethnic, and sex bias?

B. Multiple-Choice Items

1. Does the stem of the item present a single, clearly formulated problem?
2. Is the stem stated in simple, readable language?
3. Is the stem worded so that there is no repetition of material in the alternatives?
4. Is the stem stated in positive form, wherever possible?
5. If negative wording is used in the stem, is it emphasized (by underlining or caps)?
6. Is the intended answer correct or clearly best?
7. Are all alternatives grammatically consistent with the stem and parallel in form?
8. Are the alternatives free from verbal clues to the correct answer?
9. Are the distracters plausible and attractive to the uninformed?
10. Is the relative length of the correct answer varied, to eliminate length as a clue?

11. Has the alternative "all of the above" been avoided and "none of the above" used only when appropriate?

12. Is the position of the correct answer varied so that there is no detectable pattern?

C. True-False Items

1. Does each statement contain one central, significant idea?
2. Is the statement so precisely worded that it can be unequivocally judged true or false?
3. Are the statements brief and stated in simple language?
4. Are negative statements used sparingly and double negatives avoided?
5. Are statements of opinion attributed to some source?
6. Have specific determiners (such as, always, sometimes, may) and other clues (such as, length) been avoided?

D. Matching Items

1. Does each matching item contain only homogeneous material?
2. Is the list of items short with the brief responses on the right?
3. Is the list of responses longer or shorter than the list of premises, to provide an uneven match?
4. Do the directions clearly state the basis for matching and that the responses can be used once, more than once, or not at all?

E. Interpretive Exercises

1. Is the introductory material relevant to the learning outcomes to be measured?
2. Is the introductory material new to the examinees?
3. Is the introductory material as brief as possible?
4. Do the test items call forth the performance specified in the learning outcomes?
5. Do the test items meet the criteria of effective item writing that apply to the type of objective item being used?

F. Short-Answer Items

1. Is the item stated so that a single, brief answer is possible?
2. Has the item been stated as a direct question wherever feasible?
3. Do the words to be supplied relate to the main point of the item?
4. Are the blanks placed at the end of the statement?
5. Have extraneous clues (such as "a" or "an," and length of the blank) been avoided?
6. Where numerical answers are to be given, have the expected degree of precision and the units in which they are to be expressed been indicated?

G. Essay Test

1. Is each question restricted to the measurement of complex learning outcomes?
2. Is each question relevant to the learning outcome being measured?
3. Does each question present a clearly defined task?
4. Are all examinees directed to answer the same questions (unless the outcome requires a choice)?
5. Has ample time been allowed for answering, and has a time limit been suggested for each question?
6. Have adequate provisions been made for scoring the essay answers?

H. Performance Test

1. Have the performance outcomes to be measured been clearly specified?
2. Does the test situation reflect an appropriate degree of realism for the outcomes being measured?
3. Do the instructions clearly describe the test situation?
4. Are the observational forms well designed and appropriate for the performance being evaluated?

Index